SICILY

An Illustrated History

D0027949

ILLUSTRATED HISTORIES FROM HIPPOCRENE

Published...

Arizona
Patrick Lavin

Celtic World
Patrick Lavin

China
Yong Ho

Cracow
Zdzislaw Zygulski

England
Henry Weisser

France
Lisa Neal

Greece
Tom Stone

Ireland
Henry Weisser

Israel
David C. Gross

Italy
Joseph F. Privitera

Korea
David Rees

Mexico
Michael Burke

Paris
Elaine Mokhtefi

Poland
Iwo Cyprian Pogonowski

Poland in World War II
Andrew Hempel

Russia
Joel Carmichael

Sicily
Joseph F. Privitera

Spain
Fred James Hill

Tikal
John Montgomery

Forthcoming...

Egypt
Fred James Hill

London
Nick Awde & Robert Chester

Moscow
Kathy Murrell

Portugal
Lisa Neal

Romania
Nicholas Klepper

Venice
Lisa Neal

Vietnam
Shelton Woods

Wales
Henry Weisser

SICILY

An Illustrated History

JOSEPH F. PRIVITERA

HIPPOCRENE BOOKS, INC.

New York

ISBN 0-7818-0909-6

For information, address:
HIPPOCRENE BOOKS, INC.
171 Madison Avenue
New York, NY 10016
www.hippocrenebooks.com

Cataloging-in-Publication data available from the Library of Congress.

Printed in the United States of America.

Acknowledgment

I am indebted to Jim Oberthaler who has helped me prepare the illustrations, a dear friend who is always at my side when I need help in the physical preparation of my writings.

Sicily

Lorraine Hanson

Gem of dramatic mountains,
Protecting orange, lemon, loquat groves.
Grape arbors,
Patchwork shades of green
Of farms and pasture land
Amidst a sea of sparkling blue.
Lining the roads in Spring,
Scotch broom yellow,
Queen Anne's Lace, purple Thistle,
Morning Glories, white and pink,
And Poppies red.
While splashes of pink and purple,
The Bougainvillaea drips
Off walls, both high and steep,
New highways sweep from hill to hill,
White banners cleaving
Through the mountain tunnels,
Emerging at the other end,
Another roadway carpet.
And from the tops of hills,
Where once they sought
Protection from the pirate raids,
Ancient towns
Peer down through the clouds.

No condos here,
Ravaging the sandy beaches
Which await your call.
Then through the clouds
Majestic Etna rules it all,
Puffing away
Like Indian smoke signals,
With lava, vivid red,
Spouting down its side.
No wonder that the soil's so rich
And that the Ancients thought
The Gods were calling them.
All this and Doric temples, too,
And Roman villas,
 Whose churches meld
The art of East and West and Saracen.
This is the gem that Sicily offers
Those who choose to greet her.

Table of Contents

Sicily

Trapani

Palermo

Milazzo

Furnari

Messina

Barcellona

San Fratello

Corleone

Nicosia

Catania

Agrigento

Syracuse

Preface

I have purposely given larger treatment to three sections of this history—the Ancient Greek, the Saracen, and the Norman—for they are the most significant in shaping the soul of Sicily. They are indeed the most vital and the most interesting segments of the island's history. The fourth element, the Roman, contributed much: the idea of nationality, the Catholic religion, and the Sicilian language, the first offshoot from Vulgar Latin. Otherwise, Roman domination was static; the empire viewed Sicily only as a granary to supply food for the Roman legion and as a buffer against its prime enemy, Carthage.

What followed, after the Middle Ages, was the occupation by other foreign powers, which made no contribution to the island's commerce or culture, but which continued oppression, abuse, taxation, illiteracy, and abject poverty, until the 20th century—a nefarious record that deserves no more than the starkest telling. That is the role played by Spain and its Inquisition, the fifth element. The oppression ceased when Giuseppe Garibaldi, that brave warrior against oppression, freed Sicily and Italy from the Spanish yoke.

Why then bother to recount the island's history? Because, as Goethe observed, after visiting Sicily in April 1787: "One cannot conceive of Italy without Sicily; here is the key to everything."

Introduction

As the American son of Sicilian parents, I have had a yearning to pry open Sicily's past since discovering the origin of my family name. *Privitera,* my father's name, was derived from *presbitéra,* the feminine of *presbíteros* (Greek: elder, priest, leader). Sicily was first ruled for several centuries by the Ancient Greeks, who prized it as their most beautiful and fruitful island. In the Middle Ages, it was again ruled by the Greeks, known then as Byzantines.

After the Ancient Greeks came the Romans, who left a large imprint on Sicily. Thus, my maternal grandmother's name, *Cascio,* was derived from *Cassius,* a common Roman name. It was also the name of a famous Roman general and of one of the conspirators who stabbed Julius Caesar to death.

The Arabs invaded Sicily in the early 9th century and ruled it until 1074, when they were routed by the Normans. My mother's name, *Paparcuri,* was derived from an amalgam of Greek and Arabic: *papa* (Greek: father), and *khouri* (Arabic: religious).

My curiosity was sharpened further by my wife's name, Benedetta La Marca. Benedetta was in honor of the African black who was sold into slavery, brought to Sicily, and, as St. Benedict, became the patron saint of San Fratello. La Marca was a Catalan name. The Catalans, too, ruled Sicily for a long time.

Curious about the Sanfratellan dialect, which sounds as much French as it does Sicilian, my wife and I did a philological analysis. We discovered that the original Sicilian spoken in San Fratello was converted, during the Middle Ages, to a Franco-Sicilian amalgam by the troops from France's Provence. They must have been stationed there in fairly large numbers, both as soldiers and settlers, when the Normans took control of Sicily. San Fratellans still speak this dialect, which is quite distinct from Sicilian and not understood by other Sicilians.

There you have it, Sicily in a nutshell, its past all squeezed into the names of its inhabitants: Greeks, Romans, Arabs, Normans, Catalonians, and Spaniards. Many settled there, and all left their imprint on the beautiful island and its people.

Trinacria

THE GREEKS

Trinacria, three-sided, the Greeks called it: an island in the Mediterranean, just under 10,000 square miles, barely larger than nearby Sardinia. Sicily's unparalleled location—separated from Italy by a mere two miles at one point and less than 100 miles from Africa—has made the island a stepping stone between Europe and Africa, and a breakwater, dividing the Mediterranean between east and west.

Sicily's location has determined the course of its history. The list of settlers and invaders is unequalled in the annals of European history: unnamed prehistoric peoples, Sicans, Elymians, Sicels, Greeks, Carthaginians, Romans, Jews, Vandals, Saracens, Normans, Spaniards, and others. A few, like the Vandals, merely swept through, leaving no trace behind. Most stayed, for long periods or forever, contributing to the biological and cultural amalgam of the island's people, who today are Italians.

Who were the original inhabitants of Sicily? The island plainly takes its name from the *Siculi*, the Sicels. They appeared in Italy, in the toe of the boot, and are believed to have crossed the strait to Sicily in the 11th century B.C. They found on the island a people called Sicans, thought to have migrated from Spain.

It is thought that the Sicans settled in the western part of the island, while the Sicels occupied the eastern part. In the northwest corner of the island, a small territory was occupied by a people who

Greek Colonization of Italy.

seem to have made much greater advances toward a civilized life. These were the Elymi, a people who claimed a mixed descent—partly Trojan, partly Greek. Their two principal cities were Segesta, whose early remains show that Greek influence prevailed among them very early, and Eryx, where Phoenician influence was stronger.

But the Greeks were not the first to have colonized the island. As in Cyprus and in the islands of the Aegean, the Phoenicians were there before them. Phoenician settlement in Sicily began before Carthage became great, perhaps before Carthage came into being. These settlements along the coast were for trade rather than for dominion and were unable to withstand the Greek settlers who forced them to withdraw. Step by step, the Phoenicians retreated to form three considerable towns in the northwest corner of the island: Motya, Soluntum, and Panormus (Palermo).

The first presence of Ancient Greece in Sicily is the foundation in 735 B.C. of Naxos by the Chalcidians of Euboea, the Greek island in western Aegean. Located on the east coast of the island, the site is a promontory immediately below Taurmenium (Taormina). The following year Corinth began its system of settlements by founding Syracuse. From the next 150 years, Greek settlement in the island progressed steadily.

The east coast, nearest to Greece and richest in good harbors, was occupied first. There, between Naxos and Syracuse, arose the Ionian cities of Leontini and Catania (728 B.C.). Settlement on the southwestern coast began about 688 B.C. with the joint Cretan and Rhodian settlement of Gela, and went on to include Selinus, Kamarina, and, in 582 B.C., Akragas (Agrigento), which became the second largest city of Hellenic Sicily. Zancle (Messina) was founded at the northeastern corner, opposite the Italian mainland and commanding the strait.

Then nearly all of the east coast, a great part of the south coast, and a much smaller part of the north of Sicily passed into the hands of Greek settlers. The Greek element began to dominate the island. Among the early inhabitants, the Sicels were already becoming adopted Greeks. Many of them gradually became cultivators of the soil under Greek masters. But there were also independent Sicel towns in the interior: Henna (Enna, Castrogiovanni), for example, was the special seat of the worship of Demeter and her daughter.

The 7th and the early part of the 6th centuries B.C. were a time in which the Greek cities of Sicily had their full share in the general prosperity of Greek colonies everywhere. For a while they outstripped the cities of old Greece. Politically, these settlements became aristocratic kingdoms, though civil dissension led to the early rise of tyrants. The most famous, if not the first, was Phalaris of Akragas (Agrigento), who clearly rose to power very soon after the foundation of the settlement. Under his rule, the city sprang to pre-eminence in Sicily, and he was the first Siceliot (Sicilian Greek) ruler to hold dominion over two Greek cities, Akragas and Himera.

This period saw prosperity and intellectual progress. The adoption of many of Sicily's local traditions and beliefs gave the intellectual life of the island a character distinct from that of Hellenic Greece. The line of Siceliot poets began early, and Stesichorus of Himera (*c.* 632–556 B.C.) holds a great place among Greek lyric poets. The architecture and sculpture of this age have left some of their most remarkable monuments among the Greek cities of Sicily. The remains of the old temples of Selinus show the Doric style in its earlier state. In this period, too, begins the fine series of Sicilian coins.

By the 6th century B.C., the Phoenician settlements in Sicily had become dependent on Carthage, whose growing power began

Tetradrachm, Akragas, before
middle of 5th century B.C.

Didrachm, Himera,
c. 480–470 B.C.

Decadrachm, Syracuse, Dionysius I

Tetradrachm, Panormus,
c. 400 B.C.

Tetradrachm, "Siculo-Punic,"
c. 350 B.C.

Silver coins of Syracuse.

to threaten the Greeks in Sicily. Meanwhile, the growth of the tyrannies in Greek cities was beginning to group several towns under one master.

However, none of these tyrannies was long-lived. In Akragas (Agrigento), Thero's power fell to pieces under his son, Thasydaeus. The freedom of Syracuse was won by a combined movement of Greeks and Sicels in 467 B.C., when the power of Hiero passed to his brother, Thrasybulus. The Greek cities gradually overthrew the tyrannies and readopted democracy.

About fifty years of great prosperity followed in Sicily. Art, science, and poetry had been encouraged by the tyrants. To these disciplines was added the special growth of freedom, the art of public speaking, in which the Sicilian Greeks became especially proficient. Corax was the founder of the rhetorical school of Sicily. In drama, Epicharmus (540–450 B.C.) was the founder of local Sicilian comedy. In his wake, Sophron of Syracuse introduced the *mime*, a new form of Greek poetry.

The intellectual accomplishments of free Sicily abounded. Empedocles of Akragas (490?–430 B.C.) is best known for his brilliant political career, but he was a distinguished philosopher, poet, and physician as well. Gorgias of Leontini (*c.* 485–380 B.C.) had a still more direct influence on Greek culture, fathering the technical schools of rhetoric taught in Greece. Architecture advanced as well, and the Doric style gradually lost its ancient massiveness. The temple of Syracuse, which is now the metropolitan church, belongs to the earlier days of this period. It was followed by the later temples of Silenus, among them the wonderful series of temples at Akragas, and the Temple of Apollo, which is said to have been the greatest in Sicily.

One side of a temple, dating back to the 6th century B.C., now being restored in Selinunte.

Temple of Concord in Agrigento, one of the best preserved of the Greek temples in Sicily.

ATHENS VS. TRINACRIA

One of the most critical events that affected both the Siceliots and Athens took place in the 5th century B.C. (415–413). Either out of envy, jealousy, or fear of an indomitable rival, Athens responded to the call for help from Segesta against its Greek neighbor Selinus. Its result makes it a marked epoch in Sicilian history, and the Athenian plans, if successful, would have changed the whole face of the West. Its response to Segesta's plea was remarkable for the vast number of Greek cities engaged on both sides. The war was undertaken on behalf of Segesta but it involved the island's major city, Syracuse, which quickly became Athens' main target.

The Athenian intervention in Sicily is linked to the Peloponnesian War (431–404 B.C.). Peloponnesus is the southernmost region of Greece, a peninsula just west of Athens. The decisive struggle was fought between Sparta, Peloponnesia's principal city, and mainland Greece. The war lasted almost three decades, and was a total disaster. At its conclusion, Athens was no longer a player in the Sicilian landscape.

PHOENICIAN INVASION UNDER HANNIBAL

But before the war with Hellenic Greece was over, the Siceliots had to suffer another invasion on a vaster scale. The Phoenicians of Carthage stepped in as Segesta's ally after a long period of abstention from intervention in Sicilian affairs, and the observance of neutrality during the war between Athens and Syracuse.

The Phoenician leader was Hannibal, grandson of Hamilcar, who, in an earlier invasion in 480 B.C., had died at Himera. Hannibal sailed to Sicily in 409 B.C., at the head of a vast mercenary

A Bacchic scene on a Greek Sicilian vase that dates back to the 5th century B.C. Found in Agrigento.

force that attacked Selinus, Segesta's enemy, and stormed the town after a murderous assault of nine days. He then moved on to Himera, with the object of avenging his grandfather. Himera was stormed and 3,000 of its citizens were solemnly slaughtered on the spot where Hamilcar had died. Hannibal then returned to Carthage after an absence of only three months. The Phoenician possessions now stretched across the island from Himera to Selinus. The next victim was Akragas, against which another expedition sailed in 406 B.C. under Hannibal and Himilco. The town was sacked and its walls destroyed.

DIONYSIUS I

Dionysius, the tyrant of Syracuse, began his reign of thirty-eight years in the first months of 405 B.C. Almost at the same moment, the new Carthaginian commander, Himilco, attacked Gela and Camarina. Dionysius came to the help of Gela but was defeated. After allowing the people of both towns to take refuge in Syracuse, a peace was formally concluded at Gela. Carthage was confirmed in its possession of Selinus, Himera, and Akragas. The people of Gela and Camarina were allowed to occupy their towns as tributaries of Carthage. Leontini and Messina and all the Sicels were declared independent, while Dionysius was acknowledged as master of Syracuse. More than half of Sicily was now under Carthaginian dominion; several of the island's cities had perished, and a tyrant was established in the finest of its cities. The 5th century B.C., after its years of freedom and prosperity, ended in darkness.

The reign of Dionysius is marked by four years of war with Carthage, during which Sicily's geography was in flux. His dominion was extended into Rhegion (Reggio Calabria), in the toe of the Italian boot, and reached as far east as Greece, where he became an ally of Sparta. His relations with the nations of western Europe were wider than that of any earlier Greek. He also opened up new areas for Greek settlement on both sides of the Adriatic. Under his rule, Sicily became a power greater even than that of Hellenic Greece.

But his reign was less brilliant in art and literature, though he himself was a poet. The poet Philoxenus won fame in Sicily, while other authors of lost poems were admired in various Siceliot cities. One of the greatest losses in all Greek history is that of the writings of the Syracusan, Philistus (436–356 B.C.), who was admired as one of the greatest poets of the time. But the most remarkable intellectual movement in Sicily at this time was the influence of the Pythagorean philosophy, which still lived on in southern Italy and included the works of Plato.

DIONYSIUS II, DION, AND TIMOLEON

The tyranny of Dionysius was kept up for ten years after his death by his son, Dionysius II (c. 397–343 B.C.). It was a time of fright ful changes throughout Sicily, full of the breaking up of old landmarks, of confusion of races, and of movements of inhabitants. Several cities were abolished, including Naxos, Catania, and Leontini;

while several new ones were established: Tyndaris, Tauromenium (Taormina), and Halaca. During this period the Carthaginians also founded the fortress town of Lilybaeum to replace the loss of Motya.

The Dionysian tyranny was followed, in Syracuse, by the rule of Dion. He ruled for three years and, upon his death in 354 B.C., was succeeded by Timoleon. His successes include the immediate deliverance of Syracuse, the restoration of Sicily to freedom and Greek life, and the defense of the Greek cities against Carthage. But his greatest accomplishments were driving out all the tyrants and admitting the Sicels to the citizenship of free Syracuse.

AGATHOCLES AND PYRRHUS

The years that followed Timoleon's reign continued in the same manner, with incursions of the Carthaginians, the rise of tyrants, the loss of freedom of the principal cities, and the regaining of freedom. Some time during the African campaigns of Agathocles (361–289 B.C.), he took the title of king. He was also the first Sicilian ruler to put his name on coins.

Agathocles was followed by his son-in-law, Pyrrhus (318?–272), who stood as champion of the western Greeks against all invaders, whether Romans in Italy or Carthaginians in Sicily. Pyrrhus is said to have dreamed of kingdoms of Sicily and of Italy for his two sons. He himself reigned for two years in Sicily as a king who came to be no less hated than the tyrants. Still, as Hellenic champion in Sicily, he had no peer. He was the first Sicilian ruler to challenge Rome in its move down the peninsula toward Sicily itself. His having said that he left Sicily as a wrestling ground for Romans and Carthaginians turned out to be true, for very soon war broke out between Rome and Carthage.

SICILIAN GREECE

Carthage finally lost its bid for domination of Sicily to Rome, but the Greeks were not replaced without leaving their mark on the island and its people.

Under their rule, Sicily underwent settlement and development as an extension of Hellenic Greece, which it equaled, if not surpassed, in civilization and cultural achievement. The Greeks were the first to develop a sophisticated advanced civilization, with Sicilian cities whose stately monuments today outnumber those of Greece itself. They introduced Sicily to an agriculture far more advanced than any produced by the island's earlier inhabitants: vegetables and fruits; the olive tree and its oil; a large sheep industry, whose cheeses are still made in Sicily; the development of a fishing industry; and a concomitant lumber industry.

Greece had been a seafaring power, whose ships were supplied by the lumber found on its islands. Greece had no forests when Sicily was first developed. The trees had been downed and cut into lumber to build ships. What first drew the Greeks to Sicily was its lush, verdant forests, a primary source of material for a navy. But as the centuries passed, as in Hellenic Greece, Sicily's forests were stripped, beginning a process of deforestation that left Sicily resembling ancient Greece itself.

Though wrought by strife and war, the Siceliots nevertheless gave Sicily its first taste of democracy and the world some of the finest intellects in history: philosophers, mathematicians, scientists, poets, and dramatists. Many of the great Greek minds, including Plato, lived both in Hellenic Greece and Sicily. Two, however, were distinctly Sicilian: Empedocles and Archimedes.

Greek Sicilian vase depicting a tuna seller (3rd century B.C.).

Empedocles

Born in Akragas (Agrigento), Empedocles (492–432 B.C.) was the last of the great naturalist philosophers before Socrates. He taught that there are four elements—fire, water, earth, and air—that are composed of material particles that are indestructible. He believed there were two opposing forces in the world, harmony and discord, which act upon these lifeless elements and force the particles into varying combinations. Thus are created the multiple changes in the world.

Leader of the democratic faction of Akragas, he was offered the crown, which he refused. A turn in political fortunes drove him and his followers into exile.

Archimedes

Archimedes (287–212 B.C.) is famous for his work in geometry, physics, mechanics, and hydrostatics. He lived most of his life in his native Syracuse, where he was on intimate terms with the royal family. It is said that Hiero II asked him to determine whether a certain crown was pure gold or alloyed with silver. Archimedes was perplexed until, one day in his bath, he realized that gold and silver would displace different weights of water and that he could test the crown thus. His machines of war were so ingenious that the besieging Roman armies were held off for three years. When Syracuse was finally taken, the Roman general gave orders to spare the scientist, but Archimedes was nonetheless killed. Nine of Archimedes' treatises survive, demonstrating his discoveries in mathematics and in the physics of floating bodies.

Plato

Plato was one of the intellectuals who moved back and forth between Athens and Greece. In 407 B.C. he was a pupil and friend of Socrates. In 388 B.C. he lived for a time at the court of Dionysius the Elder, tyrant of Syracuse. On his return to Athens, he founded the Academy, the school at which he taught mathematics until his death. He made two more visits to Syracuse (367 and 361 B.C.). All of Plato's known writings have come down to us. His writings constitute one of the most influential bodies of work in the history of the human race. So subtle, searching, and wide-ranging was his thought that almost all the problems of subsequent philosophy are traceable in his dialogues.

Plato.

The Myths

There were myths, many intermingled with those of Greece; but three were Sicilian, born and nurtured on the island. The best known is that of Scylla and Charybdis, first mentioned by Homer (*Odyssey,* XII). It is the tale of the Strait of Messina, which separates the island

Scylla, *from the Fountain of Neptune by Montosorli.*

from the coast of Calabria. The currents were so treacherous that they wreaked havoc on the fragile Greek ships that navigated that strip of water. The sailors of ancient times told of two terrible monsters coming from the Ionian Sea and the Tyrrhenian Sea. Converging at that point, it was said that they would seize the sailors and devour them after having wrecked their ship.

There are many variations to this myth, but the most popular tells of Scylla, a beautiful sea nymph who was in love with the sea-god, Glaucus. Circe, her rival for his love, changed Scylla into a monster. She then lived on a rock between Italy and Sicily, on the Italian side of the strait. On the nearby Sicilian shore was the whirlpool of Charybdis. Italy's greatest dramatist, Luigi Pirandello, wrote a beautiful play in Sicilian entitled *Glaucus*, in which he brings this myth to life.

In another play, *Cyclops,* Pirandello rendered Euripides' satirical drama of the same name into Sicilian. In the legend, Polyphemus was a brutal one-eyed giant who ruled over Sicily through fear. He chewed up those who did not do obeisance to him, either raw or after boiling them in a huge kettle. Both in Euripides and Pirandello, Ulysses manages to blind the monster and escape his grasp.

Anyone who visits the city of Syracuse cannot fail to pay his respects to its ancient Arethusa Fountain. It is said that Arethusa was part of the Goddess Diana's retinue of nymphs. The hunter Alpheus was madly in love with her and hounded her. She sought refuge on the island of Ortigia, near Syracuse, where with the intervention of Diana she was turned into a spring in the city. According to a popular belief, Alpheus, in the form of a river, reaches Syracuse from Greece via an underground course that surfaces into the fountain to mingle with the waters of Arethusa.

Enter Rome

THE FIRST PUNIC WAR

During the twenty-three years of the First Punic War (264–241 B.C.), Sicily suffered greatly. The war was fought in and around the island, and its cities were taken and retaken by both powers. By the treaty that ended the war in 241 B.C., Carthage ceded all of its Sicilian possessions to Rome. Carthage's former holdings thus became the first Roman province; while that part of the island that kept a national Greek government, under Hiero II (c. 306–216 B.C.), became the first kingdom dependent on Rome. But upon Hiero's death in 216 B.C., his kingdom was added to the Roman province.

From the very beginning of its domination, Rome used Sicily as its principal bread basket. The corn of the fertile fields now fed the Roman people. The land was tilled by the thousands of slaves that Rome had gathered during its wars around the Mediterranean. Sicily became the granary of Rome, and the island's free population naturally degenerated and died out. The slaves were harshly treated, and the land was full of disorder under the corrupt rule of the Roman praetors.

These egregious conditions led to two great slave revolts in the second half of the 2nd century B.C. The first uprising lasted from 134 to 132 B.C., and the second from 102 to 99 B.C. But the evils that precipitated the slave revolt, and the increasing pirate attacks on coastal cities were outdone by the three years of government of Verres (73–70 B.C.). Verres thoroughly plundered and impoverished

Sicily, removing anything of value that took his fancy, especially works of art.

Gradually Roman culture began to replace the Greek. Roman buildings arose, especially amphitheatres. Although full citizenship was granted to the whole island, Sicily never became thoroughly Roman. No roads were constructed, so that not a single Roman milestone has been found in the whole island.

Few Roman emperors visited the island. In its provincial state, Sicily fell back more than some other provinces. The island had no internal history beyond a third revolt of slaves and bandits, which was quelled with difficulty in the days of Gallienus.

THE SICILIAN LANGUAGE

The language of Rome, Latin, gradually replaced the Greek that most people spoke. It was not the classical Latin that was spoken in Rome, however, but *Vulgar Latin*, the language of the *vulgus* (the people). By the year 1 A.D. most of the islanders spoke Vulgar Latin—a Latin, however, that was already beginning to break down into Sicilian. In fact, the Sicilian language has the distinction of being the first Romance language to have been derived from Vulgar Latin. Later, in the 13th century, a century before Dante and his compatriots used medieval Italian, Sicilian would become Italy's first literary language.

Although Sicilian is derived from Latin, it inherited a large lexicon from Greek. We cite but a few classes of examples: city names—Syracuse, Catania, Naxos, Taormina, and Messina; family names—Alessi *<Alexios,* Bronte *<Bronte,* Calogero *<Kalo Geron,* Politi *<Politis,* and Alfio *<Alpheus;* and general vocabulary—allisciari (to smooth*)* < *lissos (smooth)*, bucali (pitcher) *<baukalis (vase)*, and grasta (flower pot) < *rastra (pot)*.

22

Marble sarcophagus of Adelphia and Valerius, found in the S. Giovanni Catacomb in 1872. It shows characteristics of Roman sculpture of the 5th century A.D.

Roman Christian sarcophagus in Agrigento.

Under Teutonic Masters, and the Byzantine Empire

There follows a short period during which the Vandals took hold. Now seated in Carthage, they invaded and occupied several of the islands in the western Mediterranean: Sardinia, Corsica, the Balearic Isles, and Sicily. However, the Vandals soon lost these newly acquired possessions to the Goths.

Sicily again changed hands when the Goths were driven out of Italy in 551. Sicily was now part of the Byzantine Empire and, like the rest of Italy, was ruled by a Byzantine administrator whose headquarters were in Ravenna.

The Saracens

Sicily—A Muslim Land

The war against the Arabs in the western Mediterranean was a continuation of the Medieval Crusades against the Muslims in the Holy Land. From Africa, the Arabs had extended their dominion over Spain, where their culture became an integral part of Spanish life.

However the Arabs did not stop there. From Spain, they crossed the Pyrenees and for a period of three centuries invaded, sacked, and occupied southern France, and kept on the move across the Alps into Italy. Their presence was reported as far east as Torino, the capital of Piedmont.

Meanwhile, from northern Africa, they maintained a steady campaign against lower Italy, invading and occupying, at intervals, the Adriatic coast up to Bari, fighting the Greek Byzantines for a hold on the land.

The Arab attempts to conquer Sicily began in the 7th century, soon after the death of Mohammed in 632 A.D. A series of minor skirmishes was followed finally in 827 by a major invasion in which 10,000 men—Arabs, Berbers, and Spanish Muslims—landed at Mazzara. The total conquest of the island had begun. The ruling Byzantines fought vigorously to defend Sicily in a war that dragged on for fifty years, during which the island suffered famine and pestilence. The advance of the Arabs was slow but ferocious as the most important cities were destroyed: Palermo and Messina in 831, Ragusa in 848, Syracuse in 878, and Taormina in 903. Slowly

The Arabs invade Sicily.

a new civilization was introduced to Sicily and its Christian, Roman, and Byzantine heritage gradually receded. Sicily was now a Muslim land, a key member of the vast Mediterranean network.

As peace returned to Sicily, Palermo was rebuilt and became the seat of the emir, or lord, of the island. Palermo was now the capital of Sicily, replacing Syracuse as the island's most important city.

The Saracens represented a highly developed civilization that was superior, in many ways, to the Christian cultures of western Europe and the Mediterranean basin. Their agricultural methods were far more advanced than any found elsewhere. To wit, they built a system of irrigation that enabled Sicily to become again the most important producer of fruits and vegetables in the entire Mediterranean. The Saracens introduced a variety of agricultural products superior to any they found on the island or elsewhere in Europe: their own olive tree, which the Sicilian still call *la saracena,* the Saracen tree, which gives a richer, heavier oil than the Greek olive; the lemon, orange, and mulberry trees; the silk worm; the date, the pistachio, the carob, and the fig; and cotton, sugar cane, and the *zibibbo* grape, later exported to California from Sicily. All of these products gave Palermo the name *Conca d'Oro,* the golden conch.

Besides agriculture, a new tuna industry was introduced and prospered. Silver, lead, mercury, sulfur, and mineral oil were produced, and Sicilian salt became famous throughout Europe. The manufacture of silk and textiles became an important element in the island's economy. Under their care, Sicily became a land of plenty, replete with artistic structures and a rich Arabic literature. The Christian world decried the fall of Sicily to the Arabs and depicted it as a time of darkness and devastation. On the contrary, it was one more of good than bad.

To be sure, there were bad aspects to Saracen control of Sicily. Taxation continued to be excessive, but those taxes that were detrimental to agriculture were removed. The populace was divided

Bridge-aqueduct with some 40 arches, constructed by the Arabs in the 8th century.

into four distinct groups: the independents; the tributaries who paid taxes, but were otherwise free; the vassals who were subjugated war booty; and the serfs who slaved on the large estates. The people at the bottom of the social scale showed their scorn for their Muslim masters by calling them *sceccu* (SHEH koo), meaning donkey, a Sicilian play on the Arabic word for *sheik*.

THE SARACEN LEGACY

By the time the Normans invaded Sicily and routed the Muslim masters, the Saracens had laid their imprint on the island's mores, language, art, poetry, agriculture, and cuisine.

To this day, the Arab concept of the family still holds firm in Sicily. While some of the moral precepts may have originated with the Romans, when they did, they were reinforced by the Saracens: the *pater familias*, for example. The father is the head of the family; his word is law. No one begins to eat at the dinner table before the father is seated and begins his repast. All members of the family must address him with respect, which he repays with discipline, love, and protection. He earns the family's living, while his wife runs the household and raises the children.

For centuries, Sicilian women wore a black shawl, covering their head and part of their face. While the shawl is no longer a symbol of the Sicilian woman's place in society, it is still used in small towns and remote areas. In some you can see women seated at their doorstep, shelling peas or knitting, facing the wall but not the street, to which they give their back.

Within the family, an unmarried woman, as in the Muslim society, belongs to the ruling member of the family, the father, and, if he is gone, her brother. It is the male who decides her fate.

Sicilian literature is replete with situations in which the woman is shown graphically in that state of moral servitude. Luigi Pirandello's short story, "The Shawl," gives the reader a vivid view of the tragic ending of a woman caught in this egregious net. Does this situation still prevail? The answer is yes, in the island's interior and in many of the large centers.

Sicilian cuisine is markedly different from that of the Italian peninsula because a large part of it was introduced by the Arabs. The use of the eggplant, a ubiquitous Mediterranean vegetable is prepared in recipes first introduced by the Arabs. The same applies to the roasting of meats on spits. But above all, the desserts are Arabic: the *cannolo*, the pastry shell filled with sweet ricotta; and the *cassata*, the delicious cake filled with sweet ricotta, introduced by the Saracens as *Qas'at*. By *sciarbat*, the Arabs meant a sweet drink chilled with snow (from the mountains) and made with milk or water, fruit flavors, vanilla, and cinnamon. This became the Sicilian *sorbetto*, which fathered the ice cream of the Western world.

The Arabs created *semolina* from the durum wheat they introduced into Sicily; *couscous*, their main staple, is made from semolina. *Couscous* with fish is still served in Trapani, while in the Arab countries it is served with chicken or mutton. In fact, the Arabs who came to Sicily were Tunisians, and therefore fishermen, who prepared their *couscous* with fish. One of Sicily's most famous dishes, *pasta chi sardi*, is thought to have been invented near Syracuse by the Arab General Eufemio's cook. The cook put together pasta, sardines, wild fennel, and pine nuts to feed the troops with a single dish.

The Mattanza

One of the most profitable and colorful Sicilian industries is the harvesting of tuna, which was practiced during the Arab era at Favignana, a small island off the northwestern coast of Sicily. Literally, the word *mattanza* means the killing, the massive killing of a large school of tuna. The Italian verb "to kill" is *uccidere* or *ammazzare*, as it is in Sicilian. However, *mattanza* is derived from the Spanish verb *matar*, "to kill," and is cast in its present Italian-Sicilian form as *mattanza*. This fact indicates that the *mattanza* was introduced by Arabs who hailed from Spain.

The *mattanza* is now practiced almost as a religious rite in several parts of Italy. A small group of deft fisherman, under the direction of a *rais* (Arabic: leader), lay down a very large, weighted nylon net, to form a large chamber with a trapdoor. The fish are counted as they go by a glass partition at the bottom of the command boat and when the *rais* decides that the chamber is full, he gives his men the signal to begin raising the net. As it rises, the fish are speared and hauled aboard the ship. The catch is taken to a shed, where it is butchered, and then moved to the processing plant where it is cooked and canned in olive oil.

Poetry

There was poetry as well, some in the nascent Sicilian tongue and much in Arabic. Here is a brief random sampling of some of the most outstanding poets, whose artistic achievements in the conquered land soon matched those of other centers of learning—from Andalusia to Baghdad.

The poet longs for peace and for a past love
May Allah bless those days and nights/ that we spent in Khayf Muna...

If I were young again, we could once more be together...
—*Ibn Abdalla at-Tamini, c. 1060*

A love poem

Oh, my love, your coming and going pains my heart/ for you
   are not aware of my yearning/ admit at least that we were
   once lovers.

—Ali Al-Ballanûbi, c. 1030

A cry against the Normans who ousted the Arabs from Sicily

As the wolves run through the forests/ so do the invaders
   demolish/ what they find on our island/…Oh sea, why do
   you separate me from my homeland/…If I could only sail
   back to my beloved Sicily…

—Ibn Hamdis, c. 1090

Contentment

Come, pass the brimming glasses/ And let us toast from morn
   till night/ As we listen to the playing of the flutes/ Life
   can only be enjoyed under Sicilian skies

—Umar the Sicilian of Butera, c. 1130, Butera

Arabic Influence on the Sicilian Language

Arabic had a major influence on the Sicilian language. During its
dominance of the island, Arabic words infiltrated the mainstream
of daily activity. New words appeared to describe judicial and civil
procedures. Arabic roots also produced new words for clothing,
household utensils, and various foods, fruits, and sweets.

In many instances the Arab settlers wrought new names for
the towns they occupied. New names eventually appeared for
peaks, hills, valleys, hamlets, ravines, caves, and streams. Evidently
there were many streams at the time of the Arab rule, for many
names have the word for spring, *ayn*, in their construction: <u>ain</u>iddu,

clearwater; <u>ain</u>sarca, blue spring; <u>dain</u>amico, deep spring; and <u>gian</u>cardara, verdant spring.

Many derivatives of *qa'lah* (fortress, or stronghold) are found in the names of Sicilian cities: Caltagirone, Caltabellota, Caltanissetta, Calatafimi, Catalfano. Several towns have in their name a combination of *rahl* (inn, or hamlet) and *cali* (land), including <u>Racal</u>mari, <u>Racal</u>tavilla, and <u>Racal</u>muto. The Arabic word for mountain, *jibel*, is also found in the names of many Sicilian towns: <u>Gibil</u>canna, mountain stream; <u>Gibil</u>meri, the emir's stream; <u>Gibil</u>rossa, the stream at the peak; and <u>Gibill</u>seme, the lofty stream.

Here are some family names that are of Arabic origin: Alfieri *<al faris, a knight*; Barda *<bardaah, a saddle*; Caico *<haik, a weaver*; Cantara *<qantarah, a bridge*; LoFaso *<fas, axe*; Tabbano *<tabban, straw*; and Zappala *<izzb'Allah, Allah's honor*.

The following is a small sample of the many Arabic words that infiltrated daily life: <u>burnia</u>, a jar *<bumiah, a jar*; <u>cantaru</u>, dry measure (100 lbs) < *qintar, standard of weight;* <u>cassata</u>, sweet ricotta cake < *qashatah, cream*; and <u>tabbutu</u>, coffin < *tabut, coffin.*

The Normans

CRUSADE TO THE SOUTH

In just over a century, the Normans conquered Southern Italy and Sicily, a conquest no less important and much more dramatic than that of England.

The Normans (North men) were Vikings who, in barely 100 years, had transformed themselves from a band of illiterate barbarians into a civilized group of Christians. Rollo led his boats up the Seine to the eastern half of what today is Normandy, where he settled and was accepted as a ruler by the French king, Charles the Simple in 911. Rollo was not the earliest of the Norman invaders; the first wave of invaders had penetrated France a half century earlier. The intention of these invaders was clearly to settle down in their new home and become Frenchmen. It is not surprising, therefore, that Rollo and his men received Christian baptism in 912.

Within a generation or two most of their Viking characteristics had begun to disappear. By 940, the old Norse tongue, while still spoken in a few isolated areas, was already forgotten at Rouen, the capital. The Normans embraced not only the language and religion of their new land but also the newly promulgated French law, which they saw as a magnificent structure on which a state could be built. This explains why the greatest Norman architects of statehood, King Henry II of England (1133–1189) and King Roger of Sicily, concentrated on building up a massive legal system.

This preoccupation with the established columns of their adopted country was also evident in the Norman attitude to religion. Being perpetual wanderers in search of new lands to settle, the medieval pilgrimage was the perfect medium for them to explore Italy, the land to the south of France.

The tale of the Normans in Italy begins at Monte Gargano, just east of Foggia, jutting some forty miles into the Adriatic. The mountain had become famed as a land of miracles in which the Archangel Michael was thought to have appeared. By the year 1016, when some forty-odd Norman pilgrims paid a visit to Gargano, its Monte Sant'Angelo had become one of the great pilgrim shrines of Europe. It was there that the Normans met Melus, a noble Lombard from Bari who had been driven into exile by the Byzantines; the latter ruled over most of southern Italy at that time. Melus appealed to the pilgrims for help in ousting the Byzantines and in restoring the Roman Church throughout the southern part of the peninsula.

Here was the chance for which they had been waiting, a rich fertile land that offered endless opportunities for making their fortune. They told Melus they would be willing to help and that they would return the following year with a group of properly armed compatriots.

The Lombards themselves had started as semi-barbarian invaders from North Germany who had settled around the middle of the 6th century in the territory that still bears their name. As all invaders from the north were wont to do, once established in the north, they began to move south, bringing large areas under their control. It was an easy move into Italy until they reached the heel and toe of the boot, which the Byzantines controlled.

The Normans kept their word and in the summer of 1017, a group of the younger sons of knights and squires accompanied by professional fighters, gamblers, and adventurers met Melus at Capua, just north of Naples. There it was decided to attack the Byzantines before they had time to assess the new situation and summon reinforcements. Thus, by September 1018, they had the Byzantines on the run. But in October the tide suddenly turned when the Lombard and Norman forces under Melus suffered a catastrophic defeat at the hands of the imperial Byzantine army, which the Emperor Basil II (958?–1025) had sent from Constantinople to assist his beleaguered subjects. With one stroke, Byzantine power had been re-established throughout lower Italy.

But the Normans had their foot in the door and continued their plunder in a land they now wished to call their own. Early in 1030, Rainulf, the head of the largest band of Normans that were now disseminated throughout the peninsula, was formally presented with the town and territory of Aversa, northwest of Naples. By playing one side against another—fomenting discord among the squabbling Greek and Lombard barons, and selling their swords to any who would hire them— the Normans were now established as a potent force in Campania. From the moment they became landowners, their whole attitude began to change. Italy was no longer just a battlefield, no longer a land to be plundered and despoiled, but one to be appropriated, developed, and enriched. Italy had, in fact, become their home.

ENTER THE HAUTEVILLES

Rainulf's repeated calls for reinforcements, brought many young Normans to southern Italy. Among those who decided to seek their fortune in about 1035 were the first of the Hauteville family who headed straight for Aversa. There they joined Rainulf's army, in service with the Prince of Capua.

Meanwhile the Byzantines continued to be harassed by the Saracens, who now dominated the entire western Mediterranean. In 846 they had raided Rome and pillaged St. Peter's. They were already the masters of Sicily. Determined that Sicily be returned to them, the Byzantines decided to invade the island. Thus some time during the late summer of 1038, the Greek army, under the command of George Maniakes, led the attack. Maniakes was a Gargantuan figure, described by one contemporary as a ten-foot giant, who struck fear in the hearts of all who beheld him.

The Greeks invaded at a time when Sicily had become increasingly fractured, a land in which the ruling emirs found themselves increasingly divided against each other. The island was ripe for invasion. It was then in the summer of 1038 that the Greeks and their Norman allies landed on Sicilian soil. Though the Saracens fought courageously, they could do little to stem the tide. Messina fell at once, and Syracuse soon followed.

But though Maniakes had managed to restore the eastern half of the island to the Christians in less than two years, he was recalled in disgrace to Constantinople by the emperor. There, without being given the opportunity of answering the charges leveled against him, he was cast into prison. The Greeks lost their momentum and morale in Sicily and slowly began the retreat back to the peninsula.

Meanwhile, the Normans had already left in disgust. Soon after the capture of Syracuse, a dispute arose over the distribution of the spoils, of which the Normans felt they were receiving less than their fair share. With the departure of all their best fighting men, followed by that of their general, there was little hope left for the Greeks. In 1040 the island reverted to Arab control.

Meanwhile, insurrection broke out in Apulia, at the heel of the peninsula. The Italians and Lombards were revolting against their Byzantine masters. Already in 1038 several Greek officials had been murdered; in 1039 the situation was near flash-point; and in 1040 Argyrus, the son of Melus, gave the signal for revolt.

By the time the news of the insurrection reached Constantinople, Emperor Michael was dying. After a wild search for a new commander to restore order, the Greeks settled on Arduin, a Lombard, whom they named military commander of Melfi, one of the principal hill-towns along the Byzantine frontier. But although Arduin spoke perfect Greek, and was professedly pro-Greek, he was a Lombard still, at a time when his fellow-Lombards were in revolt. Therefore, he did not hesitate to turn against the Greeks and battle in favor of the Lombard cause.

In March 1041, Arduin traveled secretly to Aversa. There, with the covert support of Rainulf, he made the 300 Norman stalwarts an offer they could not refuse. He would give them Melfi as their headquarters if they would join the Lombards in driving the Greeks out of the south of Italy. In addition, he would divide the conquered territory equally between them. The Normans did not need much persuading, and they accepted with alacrity.

The actions of both the Lombards and the Byzantines were fraught with intrigue and double-dealing; this resulted in the weakening of the Greek and Lombard holdings. Significantly, in September 1042, William Bras-de-Fer (The Iron-Arm), an Hauteville knight, was unanimously proclaimed leader of all the Normans in Apulia. This event marks the beginning of the control of Apulia, Calabria, and Sicily by the Hauteville family.

In following the tale of their domination of the lower peninsula and Sicily, two sons of a certain Tancred de Hauteville are of principal interest: Robert, who later came to be known as Guiscard

(Cunning), Count and Duke of Apulia; and his younger brother Roger I, who rose to the rank of Great Count of Sicily. It was Roger's son, Roger II, who ruled Sicily as Count of Sicily, Duke of Apulia, and, finally, King of Sicily (1130–1154).

Of the Hautevilles brothers, Robert Guiscard (1015?–1085) was the principal figure in the early domination of lower Italy. A chronicle of the time describes him as "a fair and blue-eyed giant, who was perhaps the most gifted soldier and statesman of his day."

There follows a series of battles and skirmishes in which the brothers extended their control over a larger area of southern Italy. Perhaps the most critical of these was the Battle of Civitate (1049–1054) because the brothers defied and did battle with a pope.

As the Normans extended their dominion, they began approaching ever closer to the papal frontiers in middle Italy, which were rather extensive during the Middle Ages. This was during an era when the actions of the papacy were more political than sacred. At one time, the pope controlled about one-third of the Italian peninsula. In 1049, the principality of Benevento was part of papal territory.

Under pressure from the Normans, Emperor Henry III (1017–1056) invested them as imperial vassals and conceded to them the insubordinate Benevento. In doing so, he either forgot or ignored the fact that, for 250 years, Benevento had been a papal property.

Pope Leo IX (1002–1054) understood that strong measures would have to be taken quickly against the Normans if anything were to be salvaged of Church property in the south of Italy. Thus, in the winter of 1050–1051, Leo traveled to Germany to discuss the matter with the emperor. Henry III agreed to send a contingent of German soldiers to help discipline the Normans. Further consultations brought into play the Lombards and Constantinople.

But the pope's quest for retribution went badly from the very start. Thanks to the machinations of Leo's old enemy, Bishop Gebhard of Eichstätt, the army that Henry had reluctantly put at his disposal was recalled before it reached the frontiers of Italy in 1053. The pope now found himself with no alternative but to do his own recruiting. Through his chancellor, he was able to procure some 700 trained Swabian infantry. As they descended through Italy in the spring of 1053, the army grew with the addition of "a vile and promiscuous multitude of Italians," as one contemporary describes it.

Meanwhile, the various Norman segments had banded together and, on June 17, 1053, Robert Guiscard and his compatriots faced the papal army on the banks of the river Fortore, near Civitate. Leo wished to wait for the arrival of the Byzantines, while the Normans, unwilling to finally raise their swords against the Vicar of Christ, and still hoping to make a peaceful settlement, sent a deputation to Leo. It was met with scorn and jeers. And so the following morning, the battle was joined. It was a bloody battle in which the German contingent refused to surrender and were killed to the last man.

But as good Christians, the Normans went before the pope and implored his forgiveness. After burying the dead, they escorted him back to Benevento. Though they treated him with kindness, it soon became clear that the Normans had no intention of allowing him to leave Benevento until an acceptable modus vivendi had been established.

The negotiations dragged on for nine months, after which, though protesting, Leo eventually gave his *de facto* recognition to all the Norman conquests to date. Once this agreement had been reached, there was no longer any reason to prevent his return to Rome. He accordingly left on March 12, 1054, accompanied by the Normans as far as Capua.

With the pope now checkmated, the principal target of the Normans was what remained of Byzantine Apulia, where the demoralized Greeks, already deprived of papal support, and unable to obtain the support of Emperor Henry III, were no longer capable of prolonged resistance. By the end of 1055, the Apulian centers of Oria, Nardo, and Lecce had all capitulated to Robert Guiscard.

Robert was building up his reputation and his holdings at such a fast pace, that Count Humphrey, his half-brother, fearing for his own position, hastily dispatched him back to Calabria. There Cosenza and neighboring towns fell to him.

Meanwhile, Humphrey died in the spring of 1057. Understanding that Robert was the only one qualified to be his successor, he had appointed him administrator of all of his lands and guardian of his infant son Abelard. When in August 1057, he was formally acclaimed as his brother's successor by the Normans assembled at Melfi, and all Humphrey's personal estates devolved upon him, he became the greatest landowner and the most powerful figure in all of southern Italy. It had taken him just eleven years.

No fewer than seven of Tancred de Hauteville's sons had made their mark in the peninsula. There now appeared an eighth brother, Roger, who was at his arrival some twenty-six years old. But though the youngest of the Hautevilles, he was soon to prove himself a match for any. Robert took his brother under his wing and sent him off to western Calabria, which he soon subdued.

But the partnership did not last, for Robert began to display an uncharacteristic parsimoniousness, until Roger angrily left his service and accepted the invitation of another brother, William de Hauteville, Count of the Principate. But a turning-point of his life in Italy came in 1058, when Calabria was overtaken by a terrible famine, brought on by the Normans themselves; their scorched-earth policy had left not a single crop to harvest over an immense area. The desperate populace rose against its Norman oppressors and the rebellion rapidly spread throughout Calabria. Robert Guiscard had overextended himself and, unable to cope with the uprising, sent messengers to Roger, asking him to come to his help. If he would settle the Calabrian insurrection, half of the affected territory, plus all that remained for future conquest, would be his. He and Robert would enjoy equal rights and privileges in every city and town. Roger accepted and went on to put down the insurrection.

However, the Lombards, though no longer a threat to his power, caused Robert much discomfort. Only one Lombard family of sufficient prestige and distinction was now left in Italy, the ruling family of Salerno. If he tied himself to that house, the Lombard annoyances would quickly disappear. Prince Gisulf of Salerno had an unmarried sister, Sichelgaita, whom Robert could wed if he were free of his current marriage. He succeeded in freeing himself of Alberada when he "discovered prohibited degrees of kinship." He was therefore legally still a bachelor and could marry Sichelgaita. A woman of immense build and colossal strength, she proved to be the perfect wife for Robert. And from the day of their wedding, she never left his side, taking part in all their battles attired in full combat gear.

The death of Leo IX in April 1054 threw the Church into a state of confusion. There followed the appointment of three popes, two of whom died shortly after being inducted. A third was declared illegal and went into hiding. In the year 1059, there were in effect two popes, Benedict X, who was still at large, and Pope Nicholas II. It was the latter who finally called upon the Normans to serve as his right arm and protector. The Normans responded immediately; Benedict was captured, publicly unfrocked, and imprisoned. The era of Norman-Papal friendship had now begun, with the pope's confirmation of Richard as Prince of Capua, and the investiture of Robert with the Duchy of Apulia, with Calabria, and, though he had never set foot on the island, with Sicily. This event is of immense historical importance to the Normans and the papacy for it establishes the papal imprimatur on the Norman holdings. The Hautevilles were now officially tied to the pope as his protectors. They were now the accredited dominant power of southern Italy.

SICILY

Sicily was a fertile land lying three or four miles from the mainland, the lair of Saracen pirates, under the control of the detested heathens—a plum ready to be snatched. But Reggio, the point of departure from Calabria, was still in Byzantine hands. It was the capital of Byzantine Calabria, and the Greeks would fight hard to keep it. Indeed they did. But at last, thanks to the massive siege-engines that Roger had constructed, they were forced to surrender. One moonless summer night in 1060, the Byzantines embarked secretly for Constantinople. On that night Greek political rule in Calabria came to an end, never to return.

Roger and Robert then made an experimental foray across the straits, landing one night near Messina, only to be driven back to their boats by the Saracens. In October 1060, Robert Guiscard was summoned back to Apulia in all urgency. The Greeks had sent back a new army to Apulia, which by the end of the year managed to recapture much of the east coast. The Sicilian operation had to be postponed.

But Roger was not put off so easily. He returned to his headquarters in Mileto, Calabria. In the second week of February 1061,

Ibn at-Timnah, one of the three emirs who controlled Sicily, arrived in person to seek Roger's aid in defeating the other two emirs. In return, Roger would be given control of eastern Sicily.

Roger agreed and assembled a force of 160 knights and several hundred foot-soldiers, together with a small fleet. Accompanied by Ibn at-Timnah, he took Milazzo and then moved on to Messina. But there they were surprised by the fierce defense of the men and women of the city. The invading army's retreat, a few minutes later, turned into a desperate flight, with the Messinans in hot pursuit. They managed to get back to the fleet which, once under way, was intercepted by a Saracen fleet from Messina. In the ensuing battle one Norman ship was lost, while the other one barely managed to get back to Reggio, battered and exhausted.

Meanwhile, Robert Guiscard's campaign in Apulia had been successful. With the Byzantines repelled, he went to join his brother in Melfi in May. There they decided to strike again, but to alter their route and take the Saracens by surprise. In the middle of May 1061, Roger managed to accomplish this part of the plan even before Robert had followed with reinforcements.

It was over almost as soon as it had begun. On his arrival the Duke of Apulia rode in triumph through a largely deserted Messina. Most of the Muslim population had managed to escape into the hinterland.

They no sooner seized control of Messina than they began working night and day to fortify it. When the work was done Ibn at-Timnah was back with the same proposal. He would give the Normans effective control of all eastern Sicily, with the whole length of the vital coastline facing the mainland. He would also provide guides, interpreters, weapons, food, and necessary supplies. All he asked for was the routing of the other two emirs. Robert agreed readily and led his army forth again, with Roger and Ibn at-Timnah riding at his side, on the next stage of his Sicilian adventure.

Rometta, a superb natural stronghold, which commanded the mountain passes to Messina, was the next goal. The city's governor was still loyal to Ibn at-Timnah and, without hesitation, handed Robert the keys to the citadel and the town. The march continued to Frazzanò, Centuripe, and Paternò, all of which were taken with little effort. The combined army then approached Enna.

Enna was among the highest and most forbidding of all the mountain fortresses of Sicily. It was the headquarters of Ibn al-Hawas. Although they were outnumbered, the Normans enjoyed an overwhelming victory. However, they were unable to reach the emir, who was safe in his citadel with his wife and 5,000 of his men. Not equipped to undertake a winter campaign, Robert Guiscard decided to withdraw.

Roger returned to Sicily in 1062. There, after a month of fruitless campaigning, he learned that his brother was up to his old tricks. The Duke of Apulia had begun to renege on the agreement he had struck with his younger brother to share his Calabrian conquests equally with him. The younger Hauteville challenged Robert and after a confrontation, Robert lost out and had to agree to share the spoils equally with Roger.

Robert returned to Apulia, while Roger went on to attack Troina. It was a painful campaign in the midst of a brutal winter in the Nèbrodi Mountains, with dwindling supplies and improper shelter. The fortress was held by a group of Greeks and Saracens who, in the comfort of good food and warmth, passed the time away drinking wine. This episode was their undoing, for Roger, aware of their somnolent status, crept up to the enemy and took control of the citadel.

PALERMO

Syracuse had been the capital of the early Greeks in Sicily. Palermo was the Muslim capital and remained Sicily's capital throughout the Norman era. It was one of the greatest commercial and cultural centers of the Muslim world. Cairo exceeded it in size; Cordova outshone it in magnificence; but Palermo was supreme for its beautiful location, perfection of climate, and exquisite amenities. It was a busy metropolis with no less than 300 mosques, countless markets, exchanges, streets of craftsmen and artisans, and one of the first paper mills in Europe. It was surrounded by parks and pleasure-gardens, water fountains, and running streams. It is estimated that 11th-century Palermo had a population of about a quarter of a million. In 1072 it was the jewel of the Arab world.

With access by land and by sea, it was almost impenetrable, or so the Normans soon came to understand. But like all great cities, it had a soft underbelly and when the Normans, through patience, self-discipline, and superiority in arms were able to penetrate it, the prize became theirs. Early in 1064, the brothers decided to waste no more time on Enna but to head straight for Palermo. Once they had the capital, the remaining pockets of resistance would fall easily.

But their beginning was inauspicious. It was almost a comic episode, for they were routed by the scourge of southern Italy, the tarantula, which attacked their men on the hill Robert had chosen to begin his assault. They continued the siege for three months but to no avail. It was like Enna all over again. So, for the second time in three years, Guiscard found himself leading a dispirited army back to Italy.

For the next four years, the Norman army in Sicily was isolated and powerless. All its verve and momentum were gone until a summer morning in 1068 when the Norman army, out on one of its regular forays south of Palermo, found its way blocked by a great Saracen army before the small town of Misilmeri. When Roger gave the signal, his men charged and the skirmish was soon over. The battle of Misilmeri broke the back of Saracen resistance in Sicily. Ayub, the new leader of the Saracen forces, had staked not only his army but his whole political and military reputation on its outcome, and he had lost. With what remained of his following he fled back to Africa, never to return, leaving the island in total confusion and its Muslim population in despair. Their army shattered and their leaders gone, the Muslims could no longer hope to withstand Norman pressure. Palermo itself lay only ten miles or so from Misilmeri. They knew their capital was doomed.

But Roger was not ready for the capital. Its inhabitants would be expected to put up a fierce struggle, and his own forces were hardly sufficient for a siege. There was no hurry. It was better to wait for Robert to settle his affairs in Apulia and come to his aid.

Guiscard's goal was Bari—the largest, richest, and best defended of the Apulian cities. A land offensive alone would not succeed, and Robert collected a navy along the Adriatic coast.

Drawing the ships into line abreast and harnessing each one to its neighbors with great iron chains forged specially for the occasion, he formed them into a single, solid barrier that encircled the entire promontory on which the city stood. Also blocked from approaches from the landward side, Bari was now surrounded. On August 5, 1068, the great siege began. It was long and costly for both sides. The stalemate continued without remission for two-and-a-half years.

But Roger came to help just in time, and a major sea battle ensued. Of the twenty Byzantine ships involved, nine were sunk and not one was able to penetrate into the harbor of Bari. The city surrendered, seeing that it could hold out no longer. On April 16, 1071, the duke rode triumphantly through the streets of Bari. Much to the Bariots' surprise, he treated them well. But then he could afford to be magnanimous. Since the time of Justinian, Bari had been Greek—capital, at one time, of a great and prosperous province. Now its days as a prized Byzantium city had come to an end. It was now Palermo's turn.

Robert headed his fleet for the Bay of Palermo. About the middle of August 1071, Roger arrived with the bulk of the Norman army outside the capital and pitched his camp a mile or two to the east of the city. The Duke of Apulia soon arrived with his fleet and gave orders for an immediate attack. The brothers executed a pre-planned pincer movement. Roger advanced northwest and Robert pressing west along the coast, moving slowly up towards the bastions of the city. The Palermitans knew that there was little if any hope of victory, even though the future of Islam in Sicily depended on their resistance.

Just four months after the fall of Bari, the Normans found themselves engaged in another siege, this time for the greatest prize of all. It must have been in the late autumn of 1071 that a combined Saracen Sicilian-African fleet appeared off the coast of Palermo ready to do battle. Robert ordered his ships to set sail to meet the enemy. Slowly the Normans gained the upper hand, until, by the end of the day, the surviving remnants of the Saracen fleet were scuttling towards Palermo. The Norman ships crashed through, and it was in the port of Palermo itself that their blazing firebrands completed the destruction of the Sicilian navy.

The siege on land continued and in January 1072, Roger's infantry attacked. The battle was long and bloody. At first, by sheer numbers and momentum, the defenders poured out from the gates and hurled themselves at their assailants. The Norman infantry was about to retreat, until Robert Guiscard flung in his waiting cavalry and saved the situation with one mighty charge. Now it was the Saracen's turn to flee, with the Normans hard on their heels.

But they were halted suddenly when the gates to the city were slammed shut. Undaunted, Robert slipped away with 300 picked troops towards the northeast, at the administrative hub of Palermo. The district was fortified but less effectively. A bitter struggle followed.

That night the defenders of Palermo knew that they had lost and, early the following morning, a delegation of notables called on the Duke of Apulia to discuss terms for the surrender of their city. Once again Robert showed himself generous in victory. There were to be no reprisals and no further looting. All Saracen lives and property would be respected. He desired their friendship and asked only their allegiance and an annual tribute, in return for which the Normans would interfere neither with the practice of the Muslim religion nor with the application of Islamic law.

On January 10, 1072, the Duke of Apulia made his formal entry into Palermo. He was followed by his brother Roger, his wife Sichelgaita, and by all the Norman chiefs who had fought with him in the campaign.

News of the fall of Palermo had led to the spontaneous capitulation of several other regions, though subjection of the island was not yet complete. Independent emirates still struggled on at Trapani and Syracuse, to say nothing of Enna. But the cleanup would come later, at a more leisurely pace.

Meanwhile, Robert Guiscard, already provisionally invested as Duke of Sicily by Pope Nicolas, claimed suzerainty over the whole island. For his own direct tenure, he reserved only Palermo, half of Messina, and half of the Val Demone, the mountainous region of the northeast. The rest was to be held by Roger, now Great Count of Sicily.

It was autumn before Robert Guiscard returned to the mainland, never to return to Sicily. As 1072 drew to a close, loaded with the riches of his new dukedom, he rode proudly back to Italy. The conquest of Sicily had been his greatest triumph. Since the first half of the 9th century, Sicily had been wholly or largely in Muslim hands, constituting the most forward outpost of Islam, from which raiders and pirates had maintained an unremitting pressure against the southern bastions of Christendom. The task of subduing them had been left for him to perform, and he had performed it with a handful of men in barely a decade. The Norman conquest of Sicily was, with the re-conquest in Spain, the first step in the immense Christian reaction against the Muslim-held lands in the southern Mediterranean, a reaction that was shortly to develop into the colossal epic of the Crusades.

Back in Italy Robert spent the rest of his days keeping his domain in order and tilting swords with the pope over Benevento. Salerno became his capital in 1070, when he ousted his Lombard brother-in-law, Gisulf.

The most ambitious undertaking of Robert's last days was his attempt to conquer Constantinople and rid himself once and for all of the hated Byzantines. But Guiscard had overextended himself and the campaign ended in failure.

It was in 1085 that his forces were stricken by the deadliest of enemies, typhoid. His ranks were decimated and he himself died on July 17, his faithful Sichelgaita at his side. His remains were taken back to Italy and buried together with other Normans in the Church of Saint Trinità in Venosa.

The two great Normans of the 11th century were Duke William of Normandy and Robert Guiscard—Duke of Apulia, Sicily, Calabria, and Salerno. A genius and an extrovert, he carved out the most extraordinary career of the Middle Ages.

GREAT COUNT ROGER I

Before leaving Sicily, Robert Guiscard had placed his brother in charge of the island. It was the fulfillment of a dream Roger had possessed from the days when he planned to invade Sicily. He was now supreme commander and principal administrator, two roles he performed with distinction.

His first task was to extend Norman authority throughout the island. This would take time, Roger knew, for he was short of reliable manpower, with only a few knights under his command. He followed the most intelligent path: to treat the Saracens kindly and with diplomacy.

Naturally security came first. In an attempt to increase his military strength, he introduced an annual period of conscription. But for the most part, the Saracens had little cause for complaint. The mosques that had originally been converted from Christian churches were now re-consecrated. But all other mosques were left open, as they had always been, for the prayers of faithful Muslims. Islamic law was still dispensed from the local courts. Arabic was declared an official language, on an equal footing with Latin, Greek, and Norman French. In local government, many provincial emirs were retained. Nowhere on the island did the Normans show any of the brutality displayed in their conquest of England during this period. As a result, Saracen resentment, so much in evidence after the fall of Palermo, was gradually overcome. Many of those who had fled to Africa came back within a year or two.

From the very beginning, then, the Great Count began to lay the foundations of a multiracial and polyglot state in which Norman, Greek, and Saracen would follow, under a centralized administration, their own cultural traditions in freedom and concord. He genuinely admired what he had seen of Muslim civilization, and particularly Islamic architecture; while his apparent interest in the Greek Church was such that at one time the new Orthodox bishops were seriously discussing the possibility of converting him. Sicily was fortunate in having a wise, sensitive ruler at this crucial point in its history.

Unlike his brother, Roger was a gifted administrator and a warrior only by necessity. In addition to establishing a form of government that brought peace and prosperity to his polyglot subjects, he was determined to bring the entire island under his control. Because Robert Guiscard had left him with a scant number of troops, he trained and made use of the gifted Saracen warriors, who now accepted him as their leader, as well as of volunteer-settlers from Calabria, northern Italy, and France. With their help he was able to bring the remaining Saracen centers under his control.

The year 1077 saw the collapse of the last two Saracen strongholds in the west, Trapani and Erice. Taormina followed in August 1079. By the end of the year, the whole Etna massif and all of Sicily north of the Agrigento-Catania line had accepted the Norman rule. On April 1, 1086, Roger's army laid siege to Agrigento, which fell on July 25. Enna followed suit one year later.

In 1094 Count Roger was sixty-three years old and, at last, the undisputed master of Sicily. In 1091, as a protection against raids from the south, he had led an expedition to Malta, which had surrendered without a struggle.

The two decades that had elapsed since the fall of the Sicilian capital had deeply affected his character. Roger had developed into a mature and responsible statesman and, despite his conquests, he had proven himself to be fundamentally a man of peace. Thus it was that Roger of Sicily had become, by the beginning of the last decade of the 11th century, the greatest prince of the south, more powerful than any ruler on the Italian mainland.

When Roger died, on June 22, 1101 in his mainland capital of Mileto, he was seventy years old. Forty-four of those years had been spent in the south, and forty had been largely devoted to the island of Sicily. The youngest of the Hautevilles, he had begun with fewer advantages than his brothers; but by the time of his death, though still only a count, he was generally reckoned as one of the foremost princes of Europe. He had transformed Sicily. Once an island despairing and demoralized, torn asunder by internecine wars, and decaying after two centuries of misrule, it had become a political entity, peaceful and prosperous, in which four races and three religions were living side by side in mutual respect and concord. It remains the greatest accomplishment of all the rulers that the island has seen over the past two millennia.

ADELAIDE

A North Italian from Liguria, Countess Adelaide had married Roger as his third wife in 1089. In 1093 she gave birth to a son, Simon; two years later, on December 22, 1095, a second son named Roger was born. When Count Roger died in 1101, Adelaide became regent. Relying principally on native Sicilians of Greek or Arab extraction, she was outstandingly successful and was able to devote much of her time to bringing up her sons. But when her elder son Simon died on September 28, 1105, it was young Roger, not yet ten years old, who became Count of Sicily.

Count Roger I had maintained his home in Calabria, in his old mainland castle at Mileto. Adelaide changed this arrangement. Feeling hemmed in by the Norman barons there, whom she disliked and distrusted, she moved her family to the capital. Palermo was the real metropolis in Sicily, a city with a population approaching 300,000, with flourishing craft centers and industries, palaces, administrative offices, arsenals, and even a mint. She was probably completely installed in Palermo by early 1112. By coming to live permanently in Palermo, Adelaide and her son were showing that they not only trusted but depended upon their Saracen subjects for the prosperity and smooth running of the state. It is important to note that while his father had been a Norman knight, Roger was first and foremost a Sicilian.

Count Roger II, for that we must now call him, enjoyed a happy boyhood in Palermo. Once free of the cares of the Regency, Adelaide was looking for a second husband. Now enormously wealthy, she attracted a number of suitors, among whom, Baldwin of Boulogne, King of Jerusalem, was accepted. Countess Adelaide sailed for the East in the summer of 1113. Immediately after their marriage, Baldwin took hold of her dowry and began paying off his enormous debts. What was left he spent recklessly.

Having soon become bored with her, he conveniently discovered that he had never formally divorced his previous wife. Her money now all spent, Baldwin had no more use for Adelaide and so shipped her off to Sicily in the summer of 1117. She died the following year and was buried in the Cathedral of Patti.

In renouncing her, Baldwin had also broken the promise he had given in their marriage contract, that, in default of further children, at his death, the Crown of Jerusalem should pass on to Roger.

KING ROGER

Barely sixteen-and-a-half when he assumed effective power, Roger needed some time to establish his authority. It was granted to him by the exodus of many of his mainland vassals, who

Christ crowning King Roger, a mosaic in the Martorana in Palermo.

Coronation mantle of King Roger.

marched off to the Crusade. Their exit brought peace to the island, which was now richer than at any time in history. Palermo was busier than ever in the past; Messina and Syracuse were boom-towns. Before flexing his muscles, Roger decided to enlarge his navy, for it meant Sicily's prosperity in peace, and its sword and shield in time of war. This early period was one in which the young count watched his power and wealth increase.

Conscious of his growing strength and now confident of his naval supremacy, he soon began to cast covetous eyes across the sea to Africa. A first foray into the African mainland ended in disaster. Roger, now twenty-seven, chose not to lead the next expedition. It therefore set sail from Marsala in July 1123, not under his command, but under that of Admiral Christodulus. This expedition also ended in disaster, for Roger and his advisers had underestimated the strength of the Africans.

He was successful, however, in helping his cousin Duke William of Apulia bring order to his holdings on the mainland. When it became clear that William and his Lombard wife could expect no children, the cousins formally agreed in 1125 that Roger would be his heir. On July 25, 1127, Duke William of Apulia died at the age of thirty. But it was not until August 22 of the following year that Roger was able to overcome the objections of Pope Honorius and be invested Duke of Apulia. As in the Guiscard's day, Apulia, Calabria, and Sicily were all united under the same ruler. Roger was still only thirty-two. And once again, the barons and the cities of Apulia rose up against their lord.

Roger was beginning to grow accustomed to this state of affairs. His task would be to succeed where his uncle Robert Guiscard had failed and to set up, for the first time in centuries, a strong and enforceable government all through the south.

In the spring of 1129 he was back on the mainland, with an army of 3,000 knights and twice that number of infantry, including archers and a regiment of Saracens. The campaign went as planned and the renegades were brought under control. In September 1129 Duke Roger, his authority at last firmly established, summoned all the bishops, abbots, and counts of Apulia and Calabria to a solemn Court at Melfi. There, each of his vassals made an oath of fealty.

Roger was finally master of southern Italy. His task was now to weld together all the Norman dominions of the south into one nation. He therefore needed a kingship, not just for its own sake but for the sake of the mystique surrounding it. But he needed the pope's blessing, for he knew that without it, his prestige would be gravely endangered. In exchange for protection offered to the papacy, Pope Anacletus issued a Bull on September 27, 1130, granting to Roger and his heirs the Crown of Sicily, Calabria, and Apulia, together with the Principality of Capua. In turn Roger pledged his homage and fealty to Pope Anacletus, together with an annual tribute of 160 ounces of gold.

On Christmas Day 1130, Count Roger II of Sicily rode to his coronation. In the cathedral awaited him the Archbishop of Palermo, the Latin hierarchy, and representatives of the Greek Church. The pope's special envoy, the Cardinal of S. Sabina, first anointed Roger with the holy oil; then Prince Robert of Capua, Roger's vassal-in-chief, laid the crown upon his head. Finally the great doors of the cathedral were flung open and, for the first time in history, the people of Sicily gazed upon their king. The aspirations of the Norman swashbucklers had come to full fruition.

Perhaps no other king in Europe had such a large revenue as Roger, and his income from Palermo reputedly exceeded what his Norman cousins collected from all of England. Visiting foreigners noted that no other prince had so peaceful and flourishing a realm

The Church of San Giovanni degli Eremiti (a former mosque).

Bell tower of the Church of S. Maria dell'Ammiraglio della Martorana (c. mid-12th century), a prime example of Norman architecture.

as the island of Sicily. Al'Idrisi, a distinguished Arab geographer, called Palermo "the greatest and finest metropolis in the world...its beauties are infinite...all around it there are plentiful channels of water and every kind of fruit. Its buildings dazzle the eye, its defenses are impregnable." Palermo was far richer and larger than the Rome, which the Normans a few years before had largely destroyed by fire. At the other end of the island Messina, from being a small village, became an important center of trade.

Roger's Sicily and that of his two successors was above all a great meeting place of different cultures. Byzantine vestments were embroidered with Arabic lettering. Latin basilica-type buildings were crowned with Greek cupolas and covered inside with beautiful mosaics, while Arab workmen devised decorations for Christian churches out of esoteric themes from Persian mythology. Books were still being written in Palermo in both Greek and Arabic. French and Latin were the languages used at court. It is said that Roger preferred the conversation of learned Saracens to that of Christian monks. The Normans brought little to Sicilian art and learning except patronage and tolerance and pleasure in other traditions. Norman civilization was not particularly original but it provided an unusual king with the taste and the money for works of art from the different cultures embedded in Sicily.

Roger's court was also a center of science. The king had a special interest in astronomy and astrology. He took pains to regulate medical teaching and compelled doctors to undergo an examination by experts in the presence of a royal official. During his reign and that of his son, William, Latin translations were made from Plato, Euclid, and Ptolemy.

Roger ruled as king another twenty-three years and, at his death in 1154, he left a peaceful, prosperous kingdom that encompassed all of lower Italy. His successors were not his equal either in intelligence or administrative ability and, under their rule, the steady disintegration of Norman Sicily began.

WILLIAM I AND WILLIAM II

Roger was succeeded to the throne by his son William, who came to be called "William the Bad" (1120–1166). He became king at a time when the barons were reaching for political power. Many of them were violent and ambitious men. Aware of the new king's weakness and inefficiency, they strove for a greater share of power. Accordingly they stirred up a movement of racial intolerance against the Saracens. There was a baronial rising in 1155, coupled with a riot in Palermo.

Five years later, the barons organized a more successful revolt during which Maio of Bari, the king's right hand man, was stabbed to death and his corpse torn to bits by a Palermo mob. Muslims had their shops pillaged and there was a general seizing of land from Arab proprietors. The Lombard settlers used the occasion to exterminate rural Muslim settlements. When William I died in 1166, one partisan observer said that only the Muslim women wept.

William II succeeded his father at the age of thirteen, his mother, Margaret of Navarre, assumed the regency. The barons were still in revolt, and Margaret had to turn to her relatives for help. Many knights were imported from her homeland in Spain, others from France. Her cousin, Stephen of Le Perche, became chief minister in 1167. He was forceful and efficient, and consequently not liked. The fact that he would not accept bribes made him yet more unpopular; even worse, he imprisoned the most notoriously corrupt of the chancery officers and had the Governor of Palermo Castle whipped publicly for working a profitable prostitution racket.

But Stephen's role as powerful minister came to an end the following year in 1168, when a general insurrection forced him to flee to Jerusalem. The Englishman Walter Offamilio seized power and had himself elected Archbishop of Palermo. Walter remained at the center of power during a comparatively tranquil period for Sicily. William came of age in 1172, but did not openly dare challenge the archbishop. Because the barons approved of the new king, he was dubbed "William the Good."

William II lived like an oriental sovereign. He had Muslim concubines and kept a bodyguard of Negro slaves; he patronized Arab poets. Although the number of Muslims in government decreased during his reign, they still dominated the finance department. At a time when Christianity was becoming increasingly intolerant, there were still mosques in Palermo and many Muslims still lived there and kept their own judges and schools. Even the Christian women in Palermo were said to have assumed the secluded habits and the dress of Arab women, while the king himself was known to have worn Moorish costumes.

William's greatest act of patronage was to build the immense Benedictine abbey of Monreale, in which Eastern and Western styles met. The nave was essentially Latin, and the arcaded cloister fitted western monastic habits; but the ornamental marble fountain and columns of the cloister were Moorish. Inside the abbey were nearly 70,000 square feet of colored mosaics that illustrate the Bible story. These mosaics were probably done by a specialist workshop imported from Greece. These works are the largest and most important ensemble of mosaics that has survived from 12th-century Europe.

Mosaic of Bible scenes in the Cathedral of Monreale, a masterpiece of Byzantine art.

The Hohenstaufens

THE GREAT FREDERICK—HALF-NORMAN, HALF-GERMAN

William the Good's contribution to Sicily's wealth and well-being was inconspicuous. He died in 1189, at the age of thirty-six, and was succeeded by his aunt Constance, posthumous daughter of Roger II, whom William had married to the Hohenstaufen King Henry of Germany. In an effort to seek diplomatic support, he had arranged this ill-considered marriage, which resulted in handing over his kingdom to a German who would use its wealth to support extraneous interests and embroil it in the perennial contest between papacy and empire.

At Palermo the eunuchs of the palace presented Henry with the keys of the Treasury and, on Christmas Day, 1194, he crowned himself King of Sicily. It took Henry no time at all to empty the treasury and send it to Germany, together with Queen Constance's dowry. This is how King Roger's jeweled vestments ended up in a Vienna museum.

But it did not take long for the country, which had so meekly accepted Henry's arrival, to break out in rebellion against him. The emperor easily put this down with the troops he had recruited for a crusade. It is said that his victims were burned alive or boiled in oil. One of the Hauteville family was said to have had a red hot crown nailed to his living head. In the middle of this repression in

1197, the emperor himself died, at the age of thirty-two. He was succeeded by his son Frederick II.

FREDERICK II, STUPOR MUNDI (1194–1250)

It is said that the reign of the Normans in Italy came to an end in the year 1200 and that may be so, for Frederick, the next King of Sicily, was on his father's side a Hohenstaufen from Swabia. But through his mother he was a Norman, and the grandson of the great King Roger I.

Frederick became King of Sicily at age three; his mother, Queen Constance, was regent. When she died in 1198, the care of her son was entrusted to Pope Innocent III. But there was little the pope could do to protect the interests of his young ward during the ensuing period, when a succession of German barons enriched themselves and took possession of Palermo and the young king. It was a time when both Muslims and Christians rebelled, and bandits roamed the land.

When Frederick took over the government in 1208, one of his first problems was to crush these bandits. But he left these problems behind in 1212, when he had to leave Sicily. He did not come back until he returned from Germany as emperor in 1220. He immediately brought order to chaos. To begin with, he had all the castles built since 1189 destroyed, for these were the new strongholds of the upstart nobles. Norman laws about feudalism were re-stated and vassals were made to present their charter for verification or rejection, while any grant obtained since 1189 was voided. Frederick restored the royal demesne and took back rights of justice that had been usurped. The barons were once again restricted and kept in place.

Frederick II.

When he summoned a parliament in 1221, the country felt a directing authority reminiscent of King Roger. Frederick imposed strict laws of personal and civil conduct. He created a state university at Naples for the training of lawyers and administrators. He had Pier della Vigna, one of his jurists, write the *Liber Augustalis,* the legal code of 1231. Whereas Roger I had allowed Lombards, Greeks, Arabs, and Franks to be judged each by their own laws, Frederick now had them judged by a unified code, promulgated in an elegant Latin.

Henceforth, only people serving the king and his court could wear swords, and no royal official was allowed to accept a gift from people under his jurisdiction. Anyone could be punished who blasphemed the name of God or the Holy Virgin. Adulterous women were to have their noses cut off, and husbands indulgent of their wives' adultery were to be publicly whipped. No one could practice medicine without government license and a university degree. Jews and Muslims were under royal protection. The Jews were allowed to give loans at up to ten percent, but for other peoples usury was a crime.

Steadily Frederick took firm hold of every aspect of life, industry, and commerce in Sicily. As a result of the chaos that had ensued during his childhood, the Sicilian economy had partially run down in the years 1190–1220; his legislation was an attempt to restore some order.

His control of agriculture showed excellent results. The king himself was the chief landowner. He exported a good deal of his own wheat to North Africa. He gave out uncultivated land with the obligation to clear it and sow wheat, and he ordained that peasants should not have their animals or agricultural implements taken for debt. Two of the industries he encouraged were silk and the processing of sugar.

Frederick tried to protect law-abiding Muslim citizens from injury or offence, but he could not tolerate the refusal of the surviving Islamic communities to be absorbed. His steady pressure on these communities may have left society more homogeneous, but only by destroying a class of small traders and an element in agriculture that was impossible to replace. Wheat production never fully recovered from this blow. Most of the industrial artisans had been Muslims, and their departure would explain a decline in the silk and sugar trades. Between 1160 and 1246, emigration and slaughter of these Muslims left wide areas wasted and empty. It is estimated that half of the village settlements that existed in the early Middle Ages disappeared for this reason.

Frederick turned against the Sicilian Arabs because they were rebels, not because of their religion. In fact the popes referred to him as a baptized sultan, for he had Saracen pages and a *seraglio*, and he employed oriental dancers to entertain his guests. Muslims accompanied him even when he visited the Holy Land and the core of his army remained the Muslim expeditionary force at Lucera in Apulia.

Although he did not mistreat the Church, the popes excommunicated him repeatedly, for he resisted the claims of the papacy to intervene in temporal affairs, and he absolutely rejected their contention that Sicily was by rights a papal fief. Moreover, he insisted that ecclesiastics were not exempt from taxes and must pay the *collecta* just as did laymen. He was king and ruled Sicily firmly, with an iron hand.

But above all, Frederick was a brilliant intellectual with an inquisitive mind. He knew the works of Maimonides, the great rabbi who had died in Cairo in 1204. He preferred to discuss religious and intellectual questions with Jewish and Muslim philosophers, whom he thought to be particularly knowledgeable.

In his personal patronage, the emperor inclined more to science than to art. He had a great desire for knowledge. Rare books and scientific instruments were the gifts he most welcomed, and a silver planetarium from the Sultan of Damascus was his most prized possession. He liked the company of astronomers and mathematicians, and his court therefore became, with Oxford and Paris, one of the centers of mathematics in Latin Europe.

Frederick was particularly interested in animals. He introduced new breeds of horses to cross with domestic strains. In Malta he reared camels and falcons and even maintained a zoo. He spent thirty years studying falcons and importing different varieties from as far away as Ireland, Bulgaria, and India. He even helped compile a treatise in Latin on their various species.

Frederick's education had taken place in Sicily rather than Germany, since he was in Sicily from the age of two to thirteen. He spoke and wrote in the Sicilian-Italian vernacular of the day. From the Troubadours of Provence, who were welcome at his court, he learned the art of writing poetry. Many Frenchmen had come to live permanently in Sicily, bringing with them the literary traditions of their homeland. In 1209 the young Frederick had married Constance of Provence, who arrived in Palermo with a train of 500 cavaliers. These influences helped make his court a creative center of literature.

Frederick wrote poetry and gathered around him a group of poets who became known as the Sicilian School. It was they who invented the sonnet form, so widely used by Dante and his contemporaries. In fact Dante refers to the poetry of Provence and to that of Frederick and his school as models that served him in forging poetry in Italian, the new literary language.

Frederick died in 1250. His last days were spent in one of his Apulian castles, surrounded by his Muslim retinue. His body was taken to Palermo for burial. He had been, in some ways, the most remarkable ruler in medieval Europe. He is remembered today by the name he was called even in his lifetime: *Stupor Mundi,* World Wonder.

Frederick said that he loved Sicily above all his other possessions, but the fact is that he was a German emperor and Sicily was but a small part of that realm. This was a fundamental change, for as long as Sicily belonged to the world of North Africa and the Levant it had been rich, but when the island was forcibly attached to western Europe it lost many economic advantages. Moreover, Sicily's geographic position, instead of being a boon, became a handicap.

Palermo, the old Muslim-Norman capital had gone into decline under his regime. Because the king rarely visited it after 1225, Palermo was left a dead city. After 1250, the Sicilian School of poets fell apart, and Tuscany took over as the most creative center of Italian literature. Sicily's rich past had come to a whimpering end.

THE SICILIAN VESPERS

Upon Frederick's death in 1250, Sicily began a long period of decline—in power, prosperity, and security. At the hands of an unruly baronage, both royal authority and civil autonomy were diminished. His death was followed by fifteen years of civil discord, in which rival contestants fought for what was left of Norman Sicily. Ten of Frederick's children and grandchildren died in prison or by violence. In the prevailing anarchy, many towns tried to annex their surrounding territory. Messina thus subdued and almost destroyed Taormina, while Palermo extended its authority eastward to Cefalù. Meantime many a feudal castle was converted

The Sicilian Vespers.

to a base for armed bands who plundered the countryside and obstructed commerce.

The royal succession became a free-for-all game of snatch and grab. Frederick's heir, Conrad IV, died in 1254 and was followed by the pope's candidate, the English king's eight-year-old son, Edmund of Lancaster, who ruled as a make-believe King of Sicily. In 1261 a Frenchman became pope and deposed Edmund for not having paid the agreed bribe; instead he chose a fellow Frenchman, Charles of Anjou, brother of the sainted French king, Louis IX.

Meanwhile, Manfred (1232–1266), Frederick's bastard son, continued the Hohenstaufen line and was crowned at Palermo in 1258. But in 1266, Charles was crowned King of Sicily by the pope and immediately set out to depose Manfred, which he did that same year. Manfred was defeated and killed at Benevento, leaving his nephew, the fourteen-year-old Conradin, as the last hope of the Hohenstaufen line. But two years later the boy was taken prisoner and publicly beheaded. Charles of Anjou was now King of the Two Sicilies.

There followed an unhappy period for Sicily. Charles of Anjou was an inordinately ambitious man who set out to conquer as much of the world as he could reach. His army was largely made up of adventurers whose first aim was land and plunder. It took some years before Charles could command the main strategic centers of Calabria and Sicily. In order to pay his knights and to give fiefs to hundreds of Frenchmen, he confiscated many large estates. French barons were appointed to control the cities, and most of the higher royal officers were Frenchmen. As a result, Angevin feudalism took on something of the aspect of a military garrison occupying a resentful province.

Equally unpopular in the eyes of the island aristocracy was that Charles centralized public life on Naples. It was there and not in

Sicily that he found his professional administrators. There, too, was the strategic base for his foreign policy. Charles therefore lavished his attention on Naples. He visited Sicily only once, in transit from Tunis. The offences against the island and his neglect of its people are endless. Sicily was bound to rebel against Charles as it had never rebelled against Frederick.

It happened on Easter Monday, at the end of March 1282, when people were gathered outside the walls of Palermo. French soldiers were searching people for arms. One soldier was seen taking liberties with a woman, something that in this society was a greater offence than political persecution. In a moment of impetuous anger he was killed; this touched off an explosion of popular vendetta and social revolution. Every stranger who could not pronounce the word *ceci* in Italian (CHEH chee), but instead gave the word a French pronunciation (SEH see) was slaughtered, and several thousand Frenchmen were said to have been killed in a few hours. Monasteries were broken into and French monks killed. Even Sicilian women thought to be pregnant by Frenchmen were ripped open. This was a popular, barbarous revolution.

Within a few weeks, Sicily had been cleared of Frenchmen. The French garrison at Messina was expelled and some of Charles's ships were burned. The whole of Sicily was now united—united in chaos.

PETER OF ARAGON

Just when and how Aragon influence became dominant is uncertain. The opposition to Charles had come to center on the King of Aragon. By amalgamating with Catalonia, Aragon had recently obtained in Barcelona one of the great ports of the Mediterranean.

Sicily, as an agricultural-pastoral country, was to Aragon an obvious source of food and an outlet for the growing textile industry of northeastern Spain.

The fact that in 1262, Peter of Aragon married Manfred's daughter Constance, the last heir of the Hohenstaufen, gave him a claim to Sicily. But only when a group of Sicilian notables requested his help, did Peter try to intervene. He accepted the invitation and landed at Trapani on August 30, five months after the Vespers. On September 4 he was acclaimed King of Sicily at Palermo. With this act, the Kingdom of the Two Sicilies was effectively severed at the straits of Messina; and Calabria, which for centuries had been closely identified with the island of Sicily, became attached to the Kingdom of Naples.

Sicily gained in one sense but lost in another from this split with Naples. She was severed from the peninsula just when Italian history was entering the golden age of Dante and Giotto. She was separated from the University of Naples and the professional jurists who had been the backbone of the Hohenstaufen monarchy. For a century, Sicily was to remain under the ban of Rome, her leaders excommunicated and her churches interdicted by a French pope who had promoted Charles. For the next four centuries, Sicily was attached not to the Italian peninsula but to Spain.

King Peter of Sicily needed all the local assistance he could obtain and, since Aragon was so remote, he was dependent on the local feudal army, which caused him to be conciliatory to the more powerful of his new subjects. Palermo was restored to its old position of primacy at the expense of Messina, which had been favored by the Angevins. At the restored parliament, Peter agreed that the island should continue as a separate kingdom and not be merged with Aragon. As was to be expected, a new Spanish feudal aristocracy began to receive land in return for military service.

One aim of the Spanish was commercial gain, so that now tax-free exports from Sicily went to Catalan as payment for the royal debts. Raw Sicilian silk was sent to be worked by Catalan weavers, with woolen cloth being imported from Spain in return. The lion's share in Sicilian trade was thus transferred from the Florentines to the Catalan merchants who had helped finance Peter's expedition.

FREDERICK III

At Peter's death in 1285, his son James insisted on remaining king of both Sicily and Aragon, and Sicilians found themselves obliged to go on providing grain, soldiers, and ships to the common fund. James had appointed a younger brother, Frederick, as his viceroy at Palermo. This Frederick had been brought to Sicily as a child and had grown up a Sicilian. Feeling that his father's decision to keep Sicily separate from Aragon should be respected, and wanting to rule the island himself, he summoned a "parliament" to debate his brother's decision. This parliament decided that the viceroy should himself become king of an independent Sicily.

The coronation of the usurper, Frederick III, took place in 1296. At his coronation, he created a number of counts and 300 new knights, thereby broadening the basis of feudalism and of his own supporters. His forty-year reign was spent mostly in warfare against Angevin Naples. The concomitant intrigues almost caused him to lose his kingdom, but Frederick was lucky to make a compromise peace in 1302 that allowed him to retain his kingdom on condition that, after his lifetime, it would be left to the Angevins.

Under Frederick, the barons became increasingly powerful. Though they were uneducated and illiterate, administration fell increasingly into their hands. Criminal jurisdiction generally had been confined to members of the royal family, but after 1297 it was granted to the senior counts and, in time, became inheritable.

Frederick III was generous and amiable by temperament. He possessed a cultivated mind and apparently wrote poetry in Catalan. Although he was a poor administrator and diplomat, his contemporaries wrote of him with enthusiasm. He was one of Dante's favorites for having defied the political intrusion of five popes.

When he died in 1337, Sicily was still independent, though just barely, and the country was poorer than when he first arrived from Spain.

THE BUBONIC PLAGUE

The plague that Genoese galleys brought to Sicily from the Levant in 1347 lasted at least six months. It is thought to have killed one person in three, and Catania and Trapani were evacuated as people fled into the hills. It certainly killed the Regent John.

The years after 1350 witnessed a general dissolution of society. Envy of the newly enriched nobility from Spain led to friction between Latin and Catalan factions. Peace was eventually reached by simple exhaustion. The young Frederick IV was captured alternately by the Latins and by the Catalans. He had to pawn the crown jewels to gain freedom. In 1372 Naples agreed to accept Sicilian independence, but only if Frederick paid an annual tribute and called himself King of Trinacria instead of King of Sicily.

The ninety years of war with the Angevins had been devastating to Sicily. Often the enemy landed large forces that burned forests and farmsteads and cut down trees and grapevines. Its aim was to exhaust the island, stop commerce, ruin the tuna fisheries, and bring agriculture to a halt. The Angevin forces had thus uprooted many of the orange groves in Palermo's *golden conch.* "Like savage beasts," it is said, they destroyed harvests, killed herds, and tried to starve out the Sicilians. Thousands died of famine, and peasant families fled from the coastal territories, to the loss of agriculture. The wonderful irrigation works, so proudly established by the Saracens, easily fell into decay. Sicily had fallen prey to greed and ambition and had become an island of hollow, frightened, and starving people.

Under the Spanish Heel

GREED, CHAOS, FAMINE

The next century and a half reads like a comic opera where kings, popes, barons, and bandits tear at each other in a grab for power, land, and money, while the poor die of indifference, neglect, poverty, and starvation.

When Frederick IV died in 1377, he left a young daughter, Maria, in the care of Artale d'Alagona, leader of the Sicilian Catalans. The melodrama begins here with a grab for the hand of the heiress. All power bases wanted her and the Sicilian kingdom: Milan; Naples; the pope, for one of his "nephews"; and the King of Aragon. D'Alagona decided to marry her to Giangaleazzo, Viscount of Milan. But before the marriage could take place, Maria was abducted, rushed to Barcelona, and married in 1390 to Martin, the young grandson of the King of Aragon.

Thence began a new invasion of Sicily. In 1392 the Spanish landed under their general, Bernardo Cabrera, who had sold off his estates in Catalonia to equip soldiers at his own expense. Of course he had to be reimbursed and reimbursement came by turning over to him the vast estates of the wealthy Chiaramonte, who was summarily decapitated. The new ruler, Martin, entitled himself *Rex Siciliae* (King of Sicily) and took over the taxation of exports and the crown rights over forests and fisheries. This second invasion of Sicily brought a substantial new wave of landowners from Spain

Italy in the 15th and 16th centuries.

who, before long, became the leading families of Sicily and filled most bishoprics and government offices.

At a time when other countries in Europe were growing in cohesion, Sicily was losing her political personality as an independent state. Martin I remained strongly under the influence of his father, who was now King of Aragon. It was the king who financed the troops in Sicily, who appointed the jobs and fiefs, and who decided about demesne lands and ecclesiastical policy. Martin thus remained an *infante* of Aragon rather than a King of Sicily. Thus it was a Spanish general and not he, who led an expedition at Sicilian expense to put down an uprising in Sardinia in 1409. And it was in Sardinia that Martin died, donating Sicily to his father like any other item of personal property. At his death the crowns of Aragon and Sicily were again united.

In 1410 the throne became vacant under the contested regency of Queen Bianca. But General Cabrera had rival ambitions for himself and defied the Queen Regent; the country again dissolved into chaos and anarchy. Revenue could not be collected, and Bianca had to rely on private borrowing. Pope John XXII, too, put in his oar by declaring that King Ladislas of Naples was the rightful sovereign of Sicily.

Meanwhile in Spain, nine delegates representing the three kingdoms of Aragon, Catalonia, and Valencia, drew up a list of six candidates. In the end they selected Ferdinand, a minor member of the ruling dynasty of Castile. In 1412 Ferdinand proclaimed himself "by the grace of God, King of Sicily," though Sicilians had not even been consulted. The pope, foiled and in a rage, excommunicated Ferdinand.

Sicily was no longer to be a residence of kings, but for 400 years was to be administered by viceroys, the first of whom was Juan de Peñafiel, Ferdinand's son. During the forty-two year reign of Alfonso of Aragon, which began in 1416, Sicily became a base for the conquest of southern Italy. It was from Sicily that he undertook an adventurous series of wars against Florence, Genoa, Milan, and Venice; it was Sicily that gave help on a scale more generous than other parts of his empire.

Alfonso has been described as a generous patron of the arts, though he hardly deserved the appellation "Magnanimous" that he was given by his fawning Spanish and Neapolitan subjects. At Catania he set up the first Sicilian university, which did little for humane studies, but confined itself mainly to training lawyers and doctors.

Under Alfonso no crime was so great that a criminal could not buy a pardon. New offices and taxes were instituted simply so that they could then be sold, and private individuals made large profits after buying permission to mint money. Alfonso's brother, the King of Navarre, and his son both received the valuable privilege of exporting Sicilian wheat tax free, and exercised this right even when Sicily was starving.

Tax gathering now could be rewarding for a few lucky individuals, because keeping accounts was thought unnecessary, or else the books could be presented twenty years late without causing undue surprise. Thus royal officials must have appropriated large sums, and must have sometimes lent the king money that they had already stolen from him.

There is little evidence that much capital or enterprise were being applied to Sicilian agriculture. Away from the coastal cities, the peasants continued to exist in the extreme conditions of either anarchy or semi-slavery. Outside the towns the only effective law was the law of the strongest. The aristocracy claimed a legal right to bind the peasants to work from sunrise to sundown, and there were severe penalties for working shorter hours and for asking for more money.

Baronial landowners insisted that their produce be sold before that of their peasants and a town had no option but to recognize the baron's monopoly on grinding wheat, making bread, slaughtering animals, and pressing wine and oil. Under this treatment, the rural areas became depopulated and, as a result, the one-time granary of Europe now began to suffer periodic famine. An independent middle class never had much chance to consolidate itself in such a society.

The monarchy had no overriding interest in civic freedom, because all too often it saw no reason to build up an anti-baronial party. On the other hand, there was the temptation that ready money could always be obtained by selling a town with its taxes and profits of jurisdiction. Even when towns could afford to buy themselves back, the king might sell them again, as was Vizzini seven times over. Some towns remained permanently in debt as a result of purchasing their freedom. Syracuse, Lentini, Sciacca, Corleone, and Cefalù were all sold into feudal servitude by Alfonso. In return for a loan to the king, the port of Marsala was given to a Spaniard and his heirs until the loan should be repaid.

Foreign merchants played a dominant role in Sicily's economy. These were mostly Spaniards, for Sicily was an important part of the Catalan economic empire and a market where Catalan cloth was exchanged for wheat. The King of Aragon not only paid some of his servants by giving them jobs and pensions in Sicily, but also settled some of his domestic debts by selling to Catalan merchants a privileged economic position on the island.

The Genoese were the next largest foreign element in the country. Being bankers as well as merchants, they could provide Alfonso with what he needed at Naples, and in return receive special privileges in Sicily. Not only the king, but also many of the landowners came to rely on Genoese credit, and so did the town of

Messina itself. In some years Genoa took more cereals and cheese from Sicily than did Spain.

Alfonso died in 1458, bestowing Naples on his illegitimate son but his other kingdoms on his brother, John. Sicily was again divorced from Naples and the mainland. In 1479, John was succeeded by Ferdinand and he, through his wife Isabella, united Aragon with Castile, thereby enlarging the Spanish empire. Sicily was now inevitably condemned to assume a small and diminishing place.

THE SPANISH INQUISITION

Sicily was to suffer enormously from the introduction of the new Spanish Inquisition. From 1487 onwards, the notorious Torquemada was sending Inquisitors to Sicily, and soon a permanent institution was properly organized with its headquarters in the royal palace at Palermo.

The expulsion of the Jews in 1492 further exemplifies the subordination of Sicily to policies decided in Spain. There were many Jews in Sicily: in some urban areas it is possible that they were a tenth of the population. In general they had kept a certain amount of religious freedom and their own schools and magistrates. They were active not simply in money-lending, but as weavers, goldsmiths, and metal workers, and in every branch of commerce. They were especially celebrated as doctors. But occasional outbursts of intolerance grew suddenly worse after 1450, and these were made more acute by the fact that private individuals and the monarch himself stood to gain from the confiscation of Jewish property.

Although the citizens of Palermo protested that the Jews were doing no harm and their expulsion would hurt trade, the orders from Spain were firm. Many Jews left for Africa and the Levant;

some even went to Rome and Naples. Even converts forfeited much of their property. The country lost some industrious citizens and a lot of capital. This lack of craftsmen and of organized credit were to rank among the chief weaknesses of the Sicilian economy.

By 1500, the king was becoming stronger in relation to the barons. There was now an organized attack on baronial privilege, especially when Ugo Moncada arrived in 1509 as viceroy to make Sicily a military base for the conquest of North Africa. The crown discovered through examination of old records that many fiefs had been obtained illegally and fiefs therefore began to be confiscated and nobles imprisoned.

A new tax in 1512 on grain exports was a blow to landowners and merchants alike. Finally there was enormous feeling against the Spanish soldiers, who when arriving back from North Africa unpaid, began to commandeer food.

As a sign of the times, a popular revolution broke out at Palermo. Cannons were stolen from the city bastions and trained on the viceroy's palace. In desperation, Moncada reduced the food taxes, but too late; he himself was lucky to escape to Messina. The soldiers, after pillaging his palace, opened its doors to the citizenry. Many of the archives were destroyed, and an orgy of theft spread throughout the capital.

For nearly a year the government was in abeyance. Eventually Moncada advised the king to try appointing an Italian viceroy. In 1517 the Count of Monteleone arrived from Naples. All now returned to normal. But not much later, Monteleone, too, was compelled to escape to Messina. His residence at Palermo was attacked, and some of his officers were castrated and thrown out of the palace windows onto the pikes of the populace. Eventually, Monteleone was restored to power and carried out a severe repression. This false start, like its predecessor, proved that the Sicilian aristocracy possessed little cohesion and no leadership and was unlikely to be able to form a significant opposition to Spain.

Ferdinand died in 1516, leaving no male heirs and was therefore succeeded by his grandson, Charles V, an Austrian Habsburg who now ruled over a Spain that no longer meant Aragon and Barcelona. The center of gravity now shifted to Castile and Cadiz. The Mediterranean would soon be less important than the Atlantic, while Sicily's role would become even more insignificant.

The Age of Darkness—
Rule of the Spanish Viceroys

THE VICEROYS

For the next 350 years, the Spanish kings ruled Sicily in absentia, through their viceroys and the many do-nothing barons who shared the viceroy's power. The Inquisition, the third power imported from Spain, answered directly to the king, and terrified peasants, artisans, the aristocracy, and the viceroy himself. This is called the Age of Darkness because those at the bottom of the social scale paid most of the taxes, and many of them were brutalized and died a premature death from hunger and disease.

The viceroys were charged with keeping the country quiet, providing cheap bread and wages for the army, putting down banditry, and collecting as much tax as the country would stand. Most of the viceroys came from the grandees of Spain who, while not considering the salary lavish, enjoyed the numerous perks that went with the office. De Spes, for example, married a local heiress and thus acquired a Sicilian county, which passed on to his family in Spain. Another viceroy, Medinaceli, was able to marry off two daughters to rich Sicilians in the 1560s.

Be it viceregal or baronial, it was a government that was steeped in corruption; this was a malady that was widespread in a society that regarded public office as a source of private advantage. Justice was for sale. Money could buy liberation from prison, or the imprisonment and torture of a private enemy. The barons, in imitation of the king and his viceroys, sold public offices in their own fiefs. Now that Castile owned Sicily, Castilian replaced Catalan as the language of administration and of social life.

There were a few revolts against the injustice of the regime but the rebellion was against individual afflictions—hunger, the aristocracy, badly distributed taxes, or the treatment by Spanish soldiers of Sicilian women.

There were parliaments, but not the kind we know today, which serve the people and write laws to guide and regulate society. These were parliaments devised to serve the best interests of those they represented. There were three houses: the ecclesiastical, the baronial, and the domanial. The first house was that of the bishops and abbots, a privileged community that claimed exemption from many of the ordinary laws of secular society. Most of its members were foreigners who lived in Spain. The military or baronial House consisted of the leading feudatories. These men were exempt from most of the taxes, and whatever tax was levied against them was passed on to their tenants. The third was the royal or domanial house, containing representatives from those towns that remained directly subject to the king and were not part of any feudal estate.

The various immunities established by the clergy, the barons, the richer towns, and richer citizens meant that taxation fell chiefly on peasants and artisans who had no parliamentary spokesman. In short, the three houses represented those classes that benefited most by Spanish rule. But the power remained in the viceroy's hands for he appointed the heads of all three houses, and had a large share in choosing most of the members. The unfairness of the system was obvious. Poor people in general, and especially in royal towns, were worst hit.

SICILY SERVES THE KING'S INTEREST

The Spanish king looked to Sicily as a source of help in his foreign undertakings. The island had no interest in his wars, yet it was forced to contribute towards them until even viceroys protested that the country could pay no more.

The viceroy himself, though paid by Sicily, was sometimes away for years as a royal ambassador or in command of Spanish forces elsewhere. Loans contracted in Ferrara and Piedmont were sent for payment to Palermo and large quantities of bullion was dispatched from Palermo to Milano for payment of troops. Great quantities of Sicilian wheat were also required to make ship's biscuit for the fleet and to serve as a bargaining counter in diplomacy. Sicilian cereals and cheese were exchanged for African slaves and gold.

In order to check the Turks and the Barbary principalities, Ferdinand and Charles used Sicily as a base from which to establish garrisons along the African coast. They also used Sicilian galleys in the Battle of Lepanto in 1571.

For the next two centuries, the Barbary "pirates" did great damage to external and even internal trade. These so-called pirates were often simply warships or privateers of an enemy power, some of Christian origin. Many of the richest Sicilian families built up fortunes out of piracy. A law of Charles V confirmed that any infidels taken at sea could be considered as slaves, and it was thought proper for the prettiest ones to be set aside for the king.

One illiterate black slave in 16th-century Sicily was eventually canonized as a Christian saint. This was St. Benedict, revered even today in San Fratello, Sicily.

The Sicilians may have been forced to supply food and fodder to feed Spain's troops and galleys, but they were never willing participants in Spain's military undertakings. Viceroy Gonzaga complained that while Sicilians would give their money gladly for the royal service, "my one difficulty is that they will not become soldiers, since it is their nature to be unwarlike."

THE BRIGANDS

It is little wonder that this miasma of corruption, abuse of power, and greed should have given rise to a brigand element. While it began as a "Robin Hood" practice of sorts, it soon deteriorated into outright thievery. Under the iron rule of the Spaniards, those at the bottom dropped even lower into ignorance, poverty, and early death. Brigandage was a legacy the hidalgos left Sicily, and it persists to this very day in the Mafia.

The brigands of the 16th and 17th centuries preyed not only on the rich but on the poor as well. The stealing of sheep was a common means of sustenance, and those who had a piece of land or enjoyed a good source of income lived in fear of seeing members of their family kidnapped for ransom.

THE BARONS

The people were plagued not only by an absentee government but by the baronage, another parasitical group created and fostered by the Spaniards and former rulers.

Barons were an outcropping of the feudal system introduced by the Arabs and reinforced by the Normans. But the class came into full bloom under Spanish rule. While the Spanish king ruled at the top directly or through his viceroy, the barons ruled at a lower level, as landowners for whom the peasants virtually worked as serfs. In effect, eighty percent of all villages and towns were under direct feudal control in the 17th century.

The barons controlled not only the economy but the law as well. They served as rulers, lawmakers, and justices. But most important of all, the nobles lacked any practical interest in agriculture even though agriculture was the source of their wealth. Disdaining an active economic role, like their Spanish overlords, they became absentee landlords attracted by the glamour of the court and the comforts of Palermo. The productivity of the soil thus did not go back into the land; it went into the towns and into the building of palaces and churches. At the same time, provincial roads were neglected and the farming community was abandoned to malaria and brigandage. Income from the land was often spent unproductively on buying the mere prestige that went with the right to call oneself a "grandee of Spain first class."

In the 15th century, Alfonso created the first marquis not of royal blood. In 1500 there were seven counts, eleven by 1550, and twenty-one by 1600. Charles V (1500–1558) created the first dukedom in 1556. Altogether, in the 1620s, there were created seven new dukedoms, seventeen marquisates, and twenty-seven new princedoms. As the fashion caught on, 102 princedoms were created in the course of the 17th century—and this out of a population of about a million.

Each baron, as he bought his way up this hierarchy, thought himself obliged to make ever greater expenditures on outward show. Each new title acquired would bring with it the need for a larger number of retainers. Clothes and liveries also became more lavish. Spanish habits created a mode of dress that, though at first ridiculed for artificiality and even effeminacy, was later adopted with enthusiasm. Tightly fitting clothes, very short coats, beards, and long hair were an early sign of Spanish influence. The expensive fashion for using carriages began to catch on, as well as the use of perfumes. Inevitably, the rivalry in splendor in which the nobles engaged led to indebtedness and financial ruin. In fact, in 1598, Viceroy Maqueda had to set up a commission empowered to take over and administer the property of the most indebted barons. The commission gave them a regulated allowance, had their estates run more efficiently, and tried to settle some of their debts.

Thus the amount of time and effort spent by the ruling elite in striving for social position was a fundamental fact in the political and economic barrenness of this society. Instead of trying to improve the economy, the nobles spent their time deciding who should walk first in a procession or who was entitled to four horses for his carriage.

The Church

There was still another such parasitical group in the Church. Because of the law of primogeniture, younger brothers and younger sons of the Sicilian aristocracy had few prospects for an independent career, and many of them had to be placed in the Church, where they constituted a powerful pillar of the established order. Their sisters for whom parents could not find aristocratic spouses followed their brothers into the Church. All came under the authority of the Spanish prelate who represented the king's ecclesiastical authority in Sicily.

In continuing defiance of the pope, the Spanish king, who appointed Sicilian bishops, maintained effective control of the Church in Sicily. The remoteness of papal authority was one reason that the rules of the Church did not always exercise control over the clergy—why, for example, so many clergy members were married, and why regulations had to be issued more than once against the serenading of nunneries by monks. Even though Pope Paul IV attacked King Philip II ("The Most Catholic King") as a heretic and once even confiscated Sicily and awarded it to the Venetians, Philip remained in control.

Under royal patronage the wealth of the Sicilian Church became notorious. The Archbishop of Monreale at one point possessed seventy-two fiefs: his annual income in 1580 was four times that of the viceroy himself. Ecclesiastical estates continued to grow and new monasteries continued to be founded, making more and more land partially or even entirely exempt from taxes. The clergy was exempt from secular courts in both civil and criminal cases. The viceroy could not override ecclesiastical rights of asylum, with the result that criminals and bandits used the churches for refuge and as a base for further activity. The clergy had a general exemption from excise taxes for its own farm produce as well as its property. Many families used this exemption as a device for escaping taxation, transferring their property to a son or a brother who was an ecclesiastic.

THE INQUISITION

For many centuries the rich sinecures of the Church were held by absentee Spanish nobles, appointed by the king. But the most vicious, evil instrument introduced into Sicily by Spain was the Inquisition. The Inquisitors were directly responsible to the king, who appointed them and used them to control and counteract the viceroy. It is they who, not long after their arrival, got rid of the very large Jewish and Muslim element, either by death or by expulsion. The Jews were the most gifted physicians and merchants on the island; while the Muslims, descendants of the 9th-century Arabs, were the last productive agriculturalists in the land. By the end of the 17th century, none were ever again found to inhabit Sicily.

With such unlimited power at its command, the Holy Office became extremely rich. It did so mostly by confiscating the possessions of its victims, many of whom were good Catholics who were openly resentful of Spain's wrongdoing and over-taxation. One result was that the Inquisition owned vast tracts of land throughout Sicily that were outside state jurisdiction and exempt from taxation. In 1577 the viceroy put the number of officers under its command at over 20,000, and it was still growing. Obviously the Inquisition had become an institution that, once it got rid of Jews, Muslims, and heretics, spent a good deal of time feathering its nest.

By the 1590s, the king at last realized this fact and ordered that the Inquisition's jurisdiction not apply to barons, nor to tax collectors and those who owed money to the state. Even higher officials of the Holy Office could no longer be protected from the royal courts if they were themselves accused of homosexuality.

THE ECONOMY

Under Spanish rule, Sicily's economy was reduced to a shambles. Whatever productivity it had displayed was drained by the demands of the viceroy and the Spanish monarch. Members of the Sicilian aristocracy had moved away from the countryside, where they had served as country farmers. They gathered in the large centers of Palermo, Messina, and Catania; there they disported themselves in imitation of the Spanish grandees.

Agriculture, whose productivity should have been cared for and overseen by the baronage, was neglected. It was heavily taxed at the source, and taxed when exported. The peasant barely managed to survive by hiding his wheat and produce from the prying eyes of the baronial owners, the Church, the viceroy, and the Inquisition.

In 1578, Viceroy Colonna wrote that "there are few kingdoms poorer than this one." The bad years apparently were becoming more frequent. Taxation was, of course, the chief complaint against the government. A large amount of cash also went overseas to Spanish owners of Sicilian property, for a large number of the aristocracy were non-resident Spaniards. Considerable sums were also transferred in the form of salaries to non-resident foreigners who held important jobs.

Most of the higher prelates were foreigners who took all or part of their salaries back to Spain. Next to taxation, this was the biggest drain on the economy. None of this money was ploughed back into Sicilian commerce or agriculture.

Where public finance bore most heavily on economic life was over the taxation of exports—wine, cheese, silk, and cereals. This drain on the economy led to hunger and five popular uprisings at Palermo between 1512 and 1560. It was a time when tens of thousands died of starvation, and some of the dead were found with their stomachs full of grass.

The standard of living had fallen to a new low since the later Middle Ages. Food had become more expensive in a world where hunger riots were never far away. In order to economize on wheat flour, the viceroy tried ordering that fashionable gentlemen should not use starch for their cuffs and collars—a cruel commentary on the selfishness, greed, and incompetence of Spanish rule in Sicily.

AGRICULTURE

Agriculture was the base for everything in Sicily. It not only provided the raw material for commerce and industry, but most of the taxes and the greater proportion of all personal income. It was also a factor in foreign policy.

In the early 16th century, Sicily exported some two million bushels of wheat in a good year. But increased taxation, together with the growing city population and the cropping of marginal lands, posed a serious challenge. Part of the problem was that rich Sicilians were too involved in their grandee manners to have provided the changes necessary for the continuing development of agriculture. The peasants were therefore left to cultivate the land as they always had, using the most primitive tools and exploiting a single area to the point of exhaustion. Two years of bad weather could suddenly throw the whole economy into disarray.

Sicily had been the most wooded area of Magna Graecia. It was for that reason that the eastern Greeks kept wanting to settle it and assume political control. Sicily must have remained well wooded throughout the Middle Ages: venison and game had been common in the markets. When these forests disappeared it is not easy to say. In the 13th century, Sicily still provided timber for shipbuilding; but, by the 17th century, there was hardly enough for local consumption.

By the middle of the 16th century, deforestation was showing its usual effects. As the soil dried out, avalanches occasionally destroyed roads, cutting off villages or even burying them, sometimes killing hundreds of people. Soil erosion gradually began to upset water control, change the course of rivers, and create regular annual floods. Fertile valleys were being crippled by the spread of marshlands and malaria. Rivers that had once provided irrigation now disappeared for most of the year. In the wet season they became torrents that carried away bridges, destroyed mills and houses, and sometimes broke down city walls. What had once been an island of lush forests and gardens was being reduced to an arid unproductive land. The economy had suffered an irreparable loss.

INDUSTRY AND THE CITIES

Wool, cotton, and silk had all been cultivated in Sicily during the Middle Ages, but Spain discouraged the development of higher quality textiles that might rival Catalan cloth. Spain also discouraged the manufacture of fine cloth. As a result domestically grown cotton continued to go overseas for manufacture, only to be imported back into Sicily as finished goods.

Much the same happened to silk. Silk weaving never recovered from the exodus of Arab workers in the 12th and 13th centuries, and of the Jews after 1492. Ninety percent of Sicilian silk was exported raw. A host of restrictive practices left the silk interest unable to compete with France and Genoa.

Palermo was the biggest city of Sicily with a population estimated at about a million in 1500. Its bloated population was reported upon by a Venetian ambassador, who described it as a parasite town where almost all the aristocracy now resided, a town that consumed most of the revenues of the island and yet despised the country districts that made its luxurious living possible.

Messina was a smaller but more mercantile and potentially richer city than Palermo. It was a great emporium for the whole Mediterranean. But Messina had some physical handicaps that cut back on its prosperity. Once in each century, Messina was devastated by earthquakes. Its trade with the Levant also suffered from the Turkish wars and Greek and African pirates. Yet the 16th century was a great period of municipal expansion in Messina.

In addition to the expansion of the two biggest cities of Sicily, there was a remarkable development of new towns and villages due to increased immigration. Of seven main villages created by these immigrants, the largest was Piana Dei Greci, where Albanians settled. These were mostly Catholics of the Greek rite, who had retained their own priests, their own language, folklore, and fashions of dress. In building new villages, the Albanians gave an impetus to a movement that, by 1600, was changing the Sicilian countryside.

THE ECONOMY AFTER 1600

The reign of Philip III (1598–1621) was a time of exceptional economic difficulty. One calamity that gravely damaged the economy at this time was the bubonic plague. In 1575 both Palermo and Messina suffered badly. One report stated that half the population of Messina had died.

Another serious infection arrived at Palermo in 1624 on ships carrying Christian slaves redeemed from Tunis. The whole of the town came to a halt. Many people died, including the viceroy himself. (Van Dyck, who was painting the viceroy, escaped overseas in time.)

When the Thirty Years War began in 1618, Sicily was required to help the Habsburg cause, another drain on the economy. As Spain approached the moment of its defeat by France, the country's demands on Sicily became greater than ever. But finally the viceroy reported that no more revenue could be found. Commerce was at a standstill and, at last, even parliament was emboldened to say that further demands could hardly be met.

Costumes of Piana dei Greci, settled by the Albanians in the 15th century. Other Albanian towns include Mezzoiuso, Palazzo, Adriano, and Contessa Entellina.

Spanish Sicily Disintegrates

THE BEGINNING OF THE END

In Sicily, as in many other parts of Europe, the last decade of the Thirty Years War was a time of political and economic crisis. Too much money had been sent overseas to pay for the war, and the economy had begun to fall apart. It is the period during which Spanish Sicily disintegrates.

THE PALERMO REVOLT OF 1647

In 1644 the quality of bread in Palermo had dropped. When Messina was forced to reduce the subsidized bread ration, there were riots. Palermo's attempt to maintain the former price and weight of bread resulted in the starving peasantry's rush into the city, thereby creating an impossible pressure on supplies. The situation was made worse by a savage drought in March and April. In the countryside there was sometimes nothing to eat except wild plants. In the towns there were beggars by the thousands sleeping out in the open. Disease began to spread. Dozens died of starvation each day.

Finally, in May, the bread ration could no longer be maintained. There was an open riot to cries of "Long live the King and down with taxes and bad government." The viceroy, Los Velez, shouted from a window of the palace that he would lift the food taxes, but the city hall was already on fire, the prisons were being opened, and the internal revenue office had been demolished. The terrified arch-bishop armed his clergy. Some aristocrats tried throwing money to the mob, but most of them fled to their country estates. Seeing himself alone, Los Velez panicked and fled to Messina.

Palermo was not alone, however, for food supply and the cost of living were also problems elsewhere. Some villages within the jurisdiction of Messina rose up against the food taxes. At Sciacca a hunger riot developed into an assault on the town hall and the destruction of the communal archives. At Girgenti the bishop barricaded himself in the episcopal palace to avoid giving up his stocks of food, but the mob broke through and terrified him into surrender. He even revealed where he kept money buried in the garden. The most angry scenes occurred in Catania where a shoemaker raised the cry of "Down with the food taxes and long live the King of Spain." Some of the nobles barely had time to escape by rope over the city walls, while the mob moved in procession around the town with the heads of their victims on sticks.

By September the revolution was over, and Palermo gave an enthusiastic welcome to the troops sent by Spain. When a new viceroy, Cardinal Trivulzio, assumed control, calm was restored. Cannons were trained upon the city, and a rigorous curfew imposed. There was peace at gunpoint, but still no solution to the basic problems of a corrupt economy that deprived the people of their daily bread.

THE REBELLION OF MESSINA

Ten viceroys ruled Sicily in the twenty-five years after 1648, during which time the government was again reduced to little more than the quest for food and revenue. Taxes were needed to keep the Spanish garrison paid and fed, otherwise they might mutiny. In addition huge sums had to be found for the empress's dowry, for the Spanish ambassador in Vienna, for an emergency in Germany, and for the Duke of Mantua.

Spain and its viceroy agreed that selling titles and privileges was a safer form of revenue. When the royal town of Patti, just west of Messina, was sold to Duke Ansalone (who would then be free to tax it at will), the outraged citizens closed the city gates against this mercenary intruder. The peremptory order from Madrid was "sell everything which can be sold and even which cannot be sold." The problem of food supply was now of outstanding importance. On the other hand, excessive taxation continued to discourage the growing of wheat. Now citizens of Palermo had to carry identity cards in order to exclude outsiders from the bread lines.

The revolution that broke out in Messina in 1674 was no hunger rebellion of the poor. Unlike the Palermo movement of 1647, this was rather a revolution of rich people who were clinging to privileges they thought necessary for their well-being. They feared the growing centralization of Spanish rule, as well as Palermo's hostility and its challenge to their rights over silk export, the highly prized product of its economy.

Finally, Palermo's attempt to deprive Messina and its dependent villages of their immunity from taxation, new taxes for the war against the Turks, and the order to disarm the town's privateer ships brought about a revolutionary decision in July 1674 to refuse entrance to the Spanish troops. Louis XIV's response to the Messinese call for help from France was to name the Duke of Vivonne, brother of his current mistress, Governor of Sicily. French troops were sent to Messina in early 1675.

In Palermo the Spanish viceroy called up the militia, but most of the units failed to appear. Others soon deserted, while many were sent home because of their complete unruliness. The captains of arms freely took bribes to exempt people from service. There were complaints that no one could be found fit to command even a company of infantry. The government had to fall back on five regiments of Spanish troops and three of German.

The viceroy was alarmed to discover that some of the nobles, as soon as they started to think that France was likely to win, showed signs of changing their allegiance. Meanwhile revenue dwindled to almost nothing, and money had to be brought in from Spain to pay for the war.

France retained her foothold in and around Messina, but little more than that. By 1677 the citizens of Messina had become disenchanted with the French. The citizens resented the billeting of French soldiery, partly because it was often unpaid but even more because it was a threat to their honor to have strange men living in their houses. Examples were reported that, in order to avoid family disgrace, wives were being poisoned by fathers and husbands for having consorted with French soldiers or for having been raped by them.

Finally when the French king decided to pull his troops out of Sicily without negotiating a peace guaranteeing Messina against the revenge of Spain and Palermo, the leading citizens of Messina fled, even going to live in Tunis and Constantinople. Messina was thus deserted by most of the senatorial families, who took with them all the money and stocks of silk that they could carry. As looting broke out, many citizens welcomed the return of Spanish troops and shed "tears of joy at being freed from the tyranny of France."

THE LAST YEARS OF SPANISH ADMINISTRATION

A new Spanish viceroy, Count Santisteban, was appointed in 1679, with orders to punish the city that had put Spain to immense expense and had caused tax revenue in Sicily to cease for three years. His first action was to pull down the town hall, plow up the site, and sow it with salt. The cathedral bell that had summoned the citizens of Messina to rebellion was melted down and was used by a Palermitan sculptor to portray the Spanish king trampling the hydra of rebellion.

Santisteban also abolished Messina university and spent the money instead on a formidable castle that commanded the town. The royal mint was transferred to Palermo, and property that belonged to rebel families was sold off.

The Duke of Uceda, who became viceroy in 1687, arrived to find a reign of violence everywhere, with bandits protected by the aristocracy and the judiciary, and commerce almost at a standstill.

Natural disasters added to the problems of government and the economy. No man-made events had quite the impact of the eruption of Mount Etna in 1669. A tongue of lava two kilometers wide flowed for over twenty-five kilometers from the central crater, crumbling the walls of Catania and filling up part of its port.

The earthquake of 1693 did even more damage, almost entirely destroying Noto and Modica, leaving Syracuse and Ragusa largely in ruins, and reducing Catania to rubble. Horrified observers told of how the earth opened up and swallowed people, and how rivers disappeared and enormous waves swamped the coastal villages. It is thought that five percent of the island's population died on this occasion, especially as infectious disease took hold.

The Bourbons

SICILY UNDER THREE NEW MASTERS

The inglorious reign of Charles II (1665–1700) ended the direct Habsburg line in Spain and Sicily, for he had no son. When the late king's testament was finally published, Spain and Sicily found themselves bequeathed to Philip V (1683–1746), the Bourbon grandson of King Louis XIV. But before any invasion or revolution could take place, an international congress at Utrecht (1713) took Sicily away from the Bourbon Philip V and gave it to his father-in-law, Victor Amedeo, the Duke of Savoy in Piedmont.

Sicily was now to be ruled by a succession of new masters: five years under the rule of Victor Amedeo and fourteen under the Austrians, to be followed by the Spanish-Bourbon rule from Naples.

The Duke of Savoy arrived in Sicily in 1713 and was crowned king in the Duomo of Palermo. Sicilians were encouraged by the thought that finally they had a king who would be residing on the island and who would take care of their well-being. But it did not happen, for Victor Amedeo's sole interest in the island was in drawing as much money and goods as possible with the least effort possible. Consequently, no attention was given to economic reform and social healing, so necessary after 300 years of Spanish misrule. He placed Piedmontese and Savoyards, strangers to the island, in the highest offices and returned back north.

But Sicily's problems did not stem solely from his indifferent rule. In order to appease Philip V of Spain for his loss of Sicily, the Congress of Utrecht allowed him to retain possession of all his lands on the island. He continued to retain personal property rights over as much as one-tenth of Sicily after surrendering his sovereignty to the Duke of Savoy. Philip's lands continued under the administration of Spanish officials and were exempt from taxation, from ordinary laws, and from military service for all Spaniards remaining in Sicily.

Spain, which was still smarting from the loss of the island, made an attempt in 1718 to regain control. When it sent the Spanish armada to Palermo, the Savoyard viceroy Maffei and his entourage fled in terror, leaving a Spanish viceroy appointed by Philip V of Spain to take over once more. The Spaniards managed to seize Taormina and Messina, but their success was short-lived, for the English interceded and defeated them in naval battles at Pachino in 1718.

Austria now entered on stage, as a result of its partnership with France, England, and Holland, in the Quadruple Alliance of August 2, 1718. As its troops charged after the Spaniards, the latter carried off grain and cattle and destroyed valuable fruit trees, setting fire to ancient olive trees.

The Austrians took control of Messina and Trapani in 1718 and, soon after that date, the Spaniards left the island in defeat. The Habsburg Emperor Charles VI of Austria became King of Sicily in 1720, holding on to the island until 1734. Order was maintained on the battle-ravaged island by a large army and German-speaking officials, who imposed huge tax payments to replenish the treasury of their Austrian masters.

THE SPANISH BOURBONS

Spain had never abandoned the idea of re-conquering Sicily. In 1734, Philip V of Spain, having allied himself to France and Piedmont, realized that he was now in a position to seize Sicily unopposed. Thus he urged his son, Charles of Bourbon, to seize Naples and Sicily. On May 15, 1734, he was proclaimed Charles III (1716–1788), King of Naples and Sicily. Once more Sicily was united with Naples, though now it was the pawn of a Bourbon prince of Spain. Its people's hope for a ruler who would reside on the island and care for their interests was immediately foiled by Charles' decision to rule his kingdom from Naples.

Life under Charles III was peaceful and the island enjoyed a twenty-five-year respite from decades of war and chaos. But the island he inherited had been devastated by two recent conquests, its land destroyed by war, and its people reduced to extreme poverty. Charles was effective in restoring power to the Sicilian parliament and in reviving the economy. He was also instrumental in enacting trade agreements with Turkey and Tunisia. But farmers were hurt when he cancelled long-term leases with no compensation to tenants for capital improvements. The resulting creation of squalid land-tenure contracts further plunged the landless farmer into despair. The growth of smaller farms ceased, while day laborers and sharecroppers were hired to farm the large estates. An overseer or *gabellotto* supervised the large estates and collected taxes for the owners in advance.

In 1759 Charles III left for Spain to assume succession to the Spanish throne, leaving his nine-year-old son, Ferdinand, as ruler of the Kingdom of Naples and Sicily, under the tutelage of a council. The island was again ruled by a viceroy at a time when it was suffering from famine, pestilence, and sacking by bandits. The

Church of Saint Sebastian in Acireale, an example of the baroque period of the 18ᵗʰ century.

large group of irate citizens who rioted in Palermo under the cry of "Bread! Bread! We want bread!" were summarily executed without the benefit of a trial.

THE VICEROYALTY OF CARACCIOLO

Never a good word could be said for the scores of viceroys who ruled Sicily on behalf of a foreign master. Their principal task was to maintain order and exact as much money and free goods as possible for use by their overseas master.

There was an exception, however, an outstanding exception in the person of the Marquis Domenico Caracciolo, who ruled Sicily with probity and justice. He was a Neapolitan, though born in Spain of a Spanish mother. Having lived in Paris and London at the height of the political and intellectual ferment, he came under the influence of men like Turgot, Diderot, and Helvétius. He was appointed as a man of the Enlightenment and as someone who had no private axe to grind. Being an honest man, possessed of courage, persistence, and sophisticated intelligence, he made a serious attempt to initiate radical reforms, the first since the 13th century.

His first move was to attack the Inquisition, which he suppressed in 1782. Caracciolo was a moderate anti-clerical, who closed some monasteries and reduced the number of feast days that required a public holiday. As a representative of the Apostolic Legate, he forbade bishops and abbots to ask papal permission before paying tax, and prohibited excommunication in cases that touched on politics. The jurisdiction of Church courts was further restricted, and he encouraged the police to ignore the right of asylum in churches.

The viceroy had only disdain for the Palermo senators' inability to live within their means, and for their addiction to ceremony.

Much to their chagrin, he reduced from over a hundred to eighteen the annual parades that they claimed as a senatorial privilege.

Caracciolo's chief target, however, was the nobility, because its 200 members had swallowed up the other one and a half million that made up Sicily's population. He found that Sicily was inhabited only by either oppressors or the oppressed, and its troubles could almost always be traced back to the tyranny of the great proprietors. If agriculture was defective, it was largely because landowners took everything out of the land and put nothing back; if law and order were weak, this was partly because they placed themselves above the law. A country could not flourish if the ruling elite despised commerce and successfully evaded taxes; nor if barons so terrified the peasantry by their relentless vendettas that no one dared appeal for government help. In Caracciolo's opinion, privilege could be justified only if there was a corresponding sense of public service, and of this the barons had very little.

Accordingly private armies and private military uniforms were declared illegal. Nobles were arrested for protecting delinquents or for browbeating local authorities and suborning witnesses. No previous viceroy had ever treated them so abruptly. Every means of influence was therefore used to make the king dismiss the terrible viceroy before it was too late.

Caracciolo had been selected for his post because, as an economist, he might find a way to do away with Sicily's poverty and make it more productive. One of the fundamental problems that lay in his path was the practice whereby those who could pay taxes, still paid nothing at all. He wanted to get rid of privileged exemptions and devise a tax system in which capacity to pay meant something. He thought that taxes could be raised by a third, without unduly burdening the country, while Sicily would be made more productive in the process.

To begin with, he placed an annual tax on carriages in order to pay for paving the streets of Palermo. There were some 800 horse-drawn carriages in the capital. The idea of making them pay an annual license fee was met with the greatest indignation. When some of the nobles refused to pay, the viceroy sent the bailiffs into their palaces to seize the best carriages and sell them off.

He turned next to the question of agricultural land, on which he demanded a fair land tax. A proper valuation of property was, he thought, an indispensable prerequisite of tax reform. Yet both nobles and ecclesiastics in the 1782 parliament formally objected to having one. Here Caracciolo came up against one of the chief pillars of the old regime. As a man of the Enlightenment, he viewed the Sicilian parliament as an institution that typified and protected waste, inefficiency, and unfairness.

Parliament would have to be reformed for it had become the mouthpiece of a tiny minority who thought that they had everything to lose from change. But the entrenched nobility fought him desperately.

Inevitably the viceroy became unpopular with many different kinds of people. To the rest of Europe, he was one of the most liked and admired of contemporary Italians, but in Sicily his charm, his intelligence, and his sense of duty were unappreciated. Caracciolo was frustrated and blocked at every turn. His vision of building aqueducts and constructing roads to link up the center of the island with the ports foundered and was forgotten.

The opposition to this fine public servant mounted to such a pitch, both in the court in Spain and in Naples, that he was honorably withdrawn by being promoted to a post of greater responsibility in Naples. He was succeeded by another Neapolitan man of the Enlightenment, Prince Caramanico. Though a competent administrator who supported the changes instituted by Caracciolo, he was unable to cement the changes in the face of the nobility's continued opposition. King Ferdinand I, in a bid for support of the conservative feudatories, even offered to revoke all the reforms of Caracciolo.

DECLINE AND FALL OF THE BOURBONS

There were riots, small and large: bread riots and the beginnings of a call for the rights of man. The French Revolution and Napoleon had repercussions in all of Italy. The ideas that had fermented in France and that had led to the death of the monarchy, had begun to reach Sicilian intellectuals and thinkers.

Among the latter, the Palermitan jurist, Francesco Paolo Di Blasi, plotted to replace the viceroy with a republican government. The plot was discovered and Di Blasi was arrested. Even though he suffered horrible torture, he refused to reveal the names of his co-conspirators. He was beheaded on May 20, 1795.

Three years later, in 1798, when threatened by the French, King Ferdinand the Fourth of Naples and the Third of Sicily (1751–1825), who in the thirty-nine years of his realm had not once visited Sicily, took refuge with his court in Palermo. He remained there in luxurious pomp and ceremony until 1802 when, with the help of the English Admiral Horatio Nelson, he was able to return to Naples.

But in 1806 he fled back to Sicily from Murat. In Palermo, when he requested a purse of 360,000 ounces of gold, the Sicilian parliament granted him only 150,000. Under pressure from the British, in 1812 the king accepted an English-based constitution, drafted by the jurist, Paolo Balsamo.

No sooner was the Napoleonic threat lifted in 1815, than King Ferdinand IV returned to his throne in Naples and abolished the constitution. On December 8, 1816, he unified his kingdom by bringing Naples and Sicily under one command, declaring himself Ferdinand of the Two Sicilies. Unable to do anything at the moment other than to use ridicule, the Sicilians turned out the following satiric piece that made the rounds throughout the island: Ferdinand, you were FOURTH and THIRD together, and now you are the FIRST and if you continue this nonsense, you'll end up being ZERO.

His proclamation as King of the Two Sicilies fostered four revolts: the first was a separatist movement (1820–1821); the second was federal in character (1848–1849); a third called for union with Italy (April 1860); while the fourth presaged the arrival of Giuseppe Garibaldi (May 1860).

Spurred on by the French Revolution, the first of these separatist movements broke out in Palermo on July 14, 1820. Rebels attacked and seized the fort of Castellamare in Palermo. Naples sent an expeditionary force under General Florestano Pepe, who met with the rebels on September 22 at Termini Imerese. He granted Sicily an autonomous government, but the action was not approved by Naples. Pepe was replaced by General Pietro Colletta, who brought the revolt to an end at Messina on March 26, 1821. (Alexis de Tocqueville, who visited Sicily in 1827, observed a deep-seated rancor over the brutal repression of the revolt.)

Ferdinand I died in 1825 and was succeeded by his son, Francesco I, who ruled until the end of 1830, with no improvement in the hostility between Naples and Sicily. In fact, in 1837, under the reign of Ferdinand II, the Sicilians blamed the cholera on the Bourbons who, they said, had malevolently spread it to their island. There were demonstrations in Syracuse and Catania and other cities, to which the Bourbons reacted by sending a military expedition commanded by the Minister of Police, the Marquis Saverio Del Carretto. His troops swept into Sicily and put a large number of Sicilians before the firing squad; among them was Salvatore Barbagallo Pittà, a prominent writer and cultural leader. Syracuse was punished by having its status as principal city of the province transferred to the city of Noto.

But the revolution was simply kept alive under cover. In 1842 the famous patriot Michele Amari published his stirring *History of the War of the Vespers*, with the apparent innocuous subtitle, *Sicilian Tales of the Thirteenth Century*. But when the authorities caught on to the fact that it contained an incitement to revolt against the Bourbons, Amari had to flee to France.

The second anti-Bourbon revolt broke out in Palermo on January 12, 1848: it used the Italian tri-color flag, with the Trinacria symbol at the center, accompanied by the singing of: "We raise the flag / With the red, green, and white / And with fire upon fire / Win we must or die." The rebels not only liberated all of Sicily but seized the impregnable Citadel of Messina. The parliament was restored and a new democratic-liberal constitution was promulgated. It placed parliament above the king, who no longer had the power to select its members or to dismiss it. Concomitantly, the king was declared deposed, remaining sovereign only of Naples. Instead Prince Alberto Amedeo of Savoy was declared King of Sicily. (There is still a street in Palermo called "Prince Alberto Amedeo.")

While this revolution lasted only sixteen months (January 12, 1848 to May 15, 1849), it brought the following words of praise from Mazzini: "Sicilians, you are great! In but a few days you have done much more for Italy, our common fatherland, than all of us together have done in two years of agitation." It is of signal importance that while the hundred Sicilian soldiers were outnumbered in a battle that was lost, they were accompanied by the Legion of the Pious Sisters, a predecessor of the Red Cross, who cared for the wounded and the families of the combatants.

King Ferdinand II (1810–1859) was named *Re Bomba* (King Bomb) for the terrible bombardment he ordered of the principal Sicilian cities. But the revolt was not over. In 1856 Francesco Bentivegna, leader of the Palermitan rebels, was put to death by a firing squad; for similar reasons, Salvatore Spinuzza was put to death in Cefalù. In 1859 Francesco Crispi, who had been condemned to death for having been one of the leaders of the revolution of 1848–1849, came to Sicily to announce the imminent arrival of Garibaldi. The same announcement was made by the Palermitan patriots who barely escaped death, Rosolino Pilo and Giovanni Corrao.

Ferdinand died on May 22, 1859 and was succeeded by his son, Francesco II, whose reign barely got under way before he had to flee the Garibaldi forces.

Francesco Crispi, during his exile in Genoa, had convinced Garibaldi to go to Sicily with a united revolutionary army. Garibaldi agreed, provided that Sicily demonstrated a positive revolutionary movement.

Such a revolt broke out in Palermo on April 4, 1860 but was overcome by the police. Two days later, an uprising broke out in Trapani, quickly followed by revolts in Marsala, Messina, Corleone, Cefalù, Misilmeri, Caltanissetta, and Agrigento. Crispi thus demonstrated to Garibaldi that the moment to act had arrived.

Giuseppe Garibaldi.

Giuseppe Garibaldi

THE BOURBONS ARE ROUTED

Born in Nice on July 4, 1807, Giuseppe Garibaldi devoted his entire life to freeing oppressed peoples. As a young man, he first joined the *Giovane Italia (*Italian Youth) and then entered the Sardinian navy. Soon after being assigned to the frigate *Euridice*, he plotted to seize the vessel and occupy the arsenal at Genoa, the moment Mazzini's Savoy expedition was to enter Piedmont. But he fled when the plot was discovered and he was condemned to death (June 3, 1834).

Escaping to South America in 1836, Garibaldi took part in the state of Rio Grande do Sul's revolt against Brazil. After a number of victorious engagements, he was taken prisoner and subjected to severe torture, from which he suffered dislocated limbs. When he regained his liberty, he returned to the war against Brazil and seized the port city of Porto Alegre.

After fighting for Uruguay's independence, Garibaldi formed a volunteer army of 3,000 men in Nice on June 24, 1848. But he was defeated by the Austrians at Custozza, near Verona, and was obliged to flee to Switzerland.

From Switzerland, Garibaldi went to Rome, where the Roman republic entrusted him with its defense against the French. He won a victory at San Pancrazio on April 30, 1849, remaining all day in the saddle, though wounded at the beginning of the battle.

The following month, Garibaldi was continuously engaged against the Bourbon troops at the Roman communes of Palestrina, Velletri, where he dispersed an army of 20,000 with only 3,000 volunteers.

But when Rome fell, Garibaldi left the city at the head of 4,000 volunteers, with the idea of joining the defenders of Venice. Thus, a spectacular retreat through central Italy began, with the armies of France, Austria, Spain, and Naples in pursuit. By his consummate generalship and the matchless endurance of his men, he managed to evade his pursuers and reach San Marino in central Italy, but with a sadly diminished force. Garibaldi and a few followers took refuge in the pine forests of Ravenna after vainly attempting to reach Venice. The Austrians were in hot pursuit, and most of his legionaries were captured and shot.

But Garibaldi was never far from the battlefield. In 1859, he fought the Austrians and defeated them at Casale, a Piedmontese commune. He returned to Como in 1860 to wed Countess Raimondi, who aided him during the campaign. But apprised of another crisis, he abandoned her immediately after the wedding and returned to Caprera. There he planned the invasion of Sicily with Crispi, the Sicilian patriot and statesman.

Assured of the protection of the British, Garibaldi began active preparations for the expedition to Marsala. At the last moment he hesitated, but Crispi succeeded in persuading him to sail from Genoa on May 5, 1860, with two vessels carrying a volunteer corps of 1,070 troops. Garibaldi landed at Marsala on May 11, under the protection of two British vessels.

On May 12, Garibaldi's dictatorship was proclaimed at Salemi in the province of Trapani; three days later, the Bourbon troops were routed at Calatafimi and at Trapani. Palermo fell on May 25, and, on June 6, 20,000 Bourbon regulars, supported by nine frigates and protected by two forts, were forced to capitulate.

Once established in Palermo, Garibaldi went on to rout the Bourbons at Milazzo on July 20. Nearby Messina fell on the same day. There, Garibaldi found a letter from King Victor Emmanuel II of Piedmont, dissuading him from invading the kingdom of Naples. Garibaldi's reply was to ask for "permission to disobey." On August 21 he crossed the Strait of Messina, won the Battle of Reggio (Calabria), and accepted the capitulation of 9,000 Bourbon troops at San Giovanni, a commune in the province of Cosenza. The Calabrians later named a peak at Aspromonte, a high ridge in the southern Apennines, Mount Garibaldi, in his honor.

Then Garibaldi led a triumphal march on to Naples. He entered Naples on September 7, while the Bourbon King Francesco fled to Gaeta, the fortified seaport. On October 1, Garibaldi routed the remnants of the Bourbon army of 40,000 men. There he issued a decree ordering the incorporation of the Bourbon Kingdom of the Two Sicilies into the Italian realm. On November 7, he accompanied Italian King Victor Emmanuel in his solemn entry into Naples; the following day, Garibaldi returned to Caprera, after disbanding his volunteers and recommending that they join the regular Italian army.

From 1862 to 1882, the last two decades of his life, Garibaldi continued to gather troops to free remnant parts of Italy not yet liberated. Popular enthusiasm induced the conservative government to propose that Garibaldi be given the sum of 40,000 liras and an annual pension of 2,000 liras, as a recompense for his services to Italy. He indignantly refused the proposal (May 27, 1875), but later accepted it when the Left was returned to power. At the same time, after having his marriage to Countess Raimondi annulled, he contracted another marriage with the mother of his children, Clelia and Manlio.

In 1880 Garibaldi went to Milan for the inauguration of a monument at Mentana, where many of his troops had been killed and captured. In 1882 he visited Naples and Palermo, but illness prevented him from being present at the 600th anniversary of the Sicilian Vespers. On June 2nd, 1882, his death at Caprera plunged Italy into mourning.

Giuseppe Garibaldi lived for seventy-five years, and he devoted much of his life to Italy's unification and freedom. He has a firm place in history as the real hero of the *Risorgimento* and as his country's greatest hero. He had the courage, dedication, and selflessness to wage war against Italy's enemy and all the enemies of freedom and liberty.

Sicily was finally liberated from the yoke of a foreign power. It was free at last to move ahead into the modern world, as a free society. It owes this to Giuseppe Garibaldi, a true hero of Sicilian history.

AFTER GARIBALDI

In October 1860, Garibaldi held a plebiscite in Sicily, which favored the formation of a united Italian nation under King Victor Emanuel. Its immediate effect was to end his dictatorship and turn over power to Count Cavour in Turin. This act offended those Sicilians for whom Garibaldi was a hero and deliverer. Even greater offence was caused when Cavour reneged on regional self-government for Sicily. He interpreted the vote as meaning acceptance by Sicilians of unconditional annexation. There was to be no Sicilian autonomy after all.

Arguing that there was not sufficient time to plan a new con-stitution, Cavour preferred to impose Piedmontese institutions on Sicily before anyone had time to object. But he knew nothing of Sicilian laws and institutions and simply assumed that they should be changed. Cavour continued to promise Sicilians that one day he would give them self-government, but in private he instructed officials to ignore Sicilian opinion.

King Victor Emanuel and his fellow Piedmontese saw themselves as coming to deliver Sicily from bondage, whereas Sicilian opinion was that on April 4, 1860 they themselves had launched the liberation of Italy. Northerners assumed that they were conferring great benefits on Sicily by annexation. They were surprised when the word "annexation" aroused anger and that their "superior" ways were not received with gratitude. The same anti-governmental feeling that originally made possible Garibaldi's success against the Bourbons was soon directed against Italy itself, and the first anniversary of the rebellion was celebrated with a riot.

The administrators who now arrived from the north had not been prepared to find a society and a language so completely different from their own. Tax collections and the police were as unpopular under northern rule as they had been under the despotic Spaniards. Particularly hated was conscription and the imposition of Piedmontese laws about compulsory service. Conscription was a special hardship in an agricultural society where women did not work the fields.

The mafia, which had existed long before, flourished after 1860 as never before. It was used by landowners to collect rents and intimidate laborers. Meanwhile, the old ruling elite cynically adopted the techniques of liberal government and became stronger than ever. With an electorate of little more than one percent, the landlords and their friends and employees were often the only voters. Anyone brave enough to challenge this conspiracy of the mafia and the ruling class was quickly brought to heel. The attempt to arrest Crispi in January 1861; the brutal assassination of General Corrao in 1863, in which the government was almost certainly implicated; and the imprisonment of Giuseppe Badia in 1865 were the ways the Sicilian aristocracy and the Piedmontese dealt with Garibaldi's main Sicilian lieutenants.

The local elite was not interested in popular education and often refused to build schools despite the law on compulsory education. Teachers were often unpaid, since the bosses had more profitable use for public money. Moreover, this kind of society had no use for land reform, an implied goal of the Garibaldi revolution, which ironically had substituted one enemy of the people for another. Sicily was now ruled by martial law. General Govone, the principal administrator, was given full powers in 1863, allowing him to hold military tribunals and to shoot people on the spot.

The Italian center of gravity, political as well as economic, was firmly located inside the triangle of Turin, Milan, and Genoa, and naturally the interests of the new Italy were therefore largely equated with those of the north. Sicily was treated as an importer of manufactured goods and an exporter of raw materials. This treatment resulted in the elimination of the thriving Sicilian silk and other textile industries, introduced and developed in the Middle Ages by the Saracens.

Under northern rule, Sicily was made to pay much higher taxes than usual. Thus an economic pace was chosen that suited the north, and to help pay for it, the island was suddenly expected to increase its tax contributions by a third. These additional taxes resulted in bankruptcies and in the loss of property by small landholders.

Food and political riots erupted throughout the island, leading to agricultural and economic paralysis and chaos as a way of life. A major revolt by Palermo was put down by the shelling of the city by the Italian navy and by the arrival of 40,000 troops. But unlike 1860, no Garibaldi arrived to support the revolt.

By the end of the century, Sicily was no better off than it had been under the Bourbons. The island was under-educated, over-taxed, neglected, and impoverished. It is not surprising that when the call for labor came from the nascent industrial societies of North and South America, over one million peasants left Sicily as fast as they could be moved in the holds of hundreds of ships. This exodus proved to be Sicily's salvation. Millions of dollars were sent by the new Americans to their relatives back home to tide them over until their lot improved.

Into the 20ᵗʰ Century

ITALY AT WAR

By miscalculation and bad judgment, Italy found itself at war with Austria, allied with England and France. In three years and three months of fighting, Italy mobilized 5.8 million men, of whom 680,000 were killed. When it came to dividing up the booty, Italy was treated as a junior partner. The negotiations in Paris gave Italy a vast tract of desert in the Libyan hinterlands and a tiny extension of Italian Somaliland in East Africa. While Sicily had made material and human contributions to the war, at its end, all it had was the names of the thousands of its sons who had lost their lives for the greater glory of a country that still treated it as an unwelcome appendage.

THE DARK AGE OF FASCISM

Vittorio de Sica's brilliant movie, *The Garden of the Finzi-Contini*, tells the tragic story of Mussolini's alliance with Nazi Germany and the treatment of Italians. De Sica's movie gives a heart-rending picture of what happened to the Jewish community—honorable, respectable Italians, who had their money and property confiscated and were forced to leave the country. Many sought refuge in the United States and several Latin American capitals; many were sent to Dachau and its ovens. When Mussolini ordered the Italian Jews rounded up, his henchmen found none in Sicily. There were none left after the genocide carried out 500 years earlier by the Spanish Inquisition.

Mussolini's treatment of Sicily was akin to the treatment its people received from other dictators of the past. As did the French, the Spaniards, and the Germans before him, he headed straight for Sicily's superior wheat, forcing the farmers to turn it over to the state at a price he had set for trade with other European countries. Otherwise it was tight control over education, economy, and the press, turning Sicily back to the darkest moments of its past.

WORLD WAR II

It was a war Sicilians prayed that Mussolini would lose, and he did lose it, ending up murdered and hanging by the heels outside a gas station in northern Italy. Sicily was in the war from 1940 to 1943, during which it suffered considerable loss of life and property. The city of Catania alone had 752 dead and over 3,000 wounded. The people wrote on the wall of one cemetery, "Long live the Duce. This is where he has lead us."

The island was occupied for thirty-eight days in 1943 (July 10 to August 17) by the Seventh American Army of General George Patton and the Eighth British Army of General Bernard Montgomery.

In 1943, finally exasperated by the unending wrongs imposed upon it by Italy's central government, Sicily created an organization entitled *Movement for Sicilian Independence,* headed by Andrea

Finocchiaro Aprile. Supported by illustrious members of society and over half a million members, it was secretly backed by the *Volunteer Army for Sicilian Independence*, which did battle with the army and the police at Randazzo on June 17, 1945 and at Caltagirone on December 29, 1945.

Finally, on May 15, 1946, Sicily was granted regional autonomy. On April 20, 1947, the Sicilian parliament was brought back to life, after ninety-eight years of silence, But the autonomy that the island received did not include progress.

Speaking for all of Sicily, the eminent historian Santi Correnti has pointed the finger at Rome for discriminating against his people. Bureaucratic mishandling closed prime markets to Sicily's agricultural products. The opening of a casino at Taormina was denied Sicily, while the four casinos at San Remo, Saint Vincent, Campione d'Italia, and Venice were allowed to prosper. A highway between Palermo and Messina, a potential boon to tourism, was not completed.

But worst of all, the government turned down a magnanimous offer made by the American company, Sverdrup and Parcel, builders of the Verrazzano Narrows Bridge of New York. The offer was to build for free a bridge across the Strait of Messina, linking Sicily to the mainland, a tie that would link Sicily closer to the mainland and its economic, industrial, and cultural life. All the company asked in payment was the collection of a small toll for a period of thirty-nine years. The offer was turned down by Rome. No reason was ever given.

Ninety percent of Italy's petroleum comes from oil wells in Ragusa and Gela, and it is refined in Augusta, Gela, and Milazzo. Nonetheless Sicilians pay a higher tax on gasoline than do the residents of northwest Italy.

SICILY AND THE MAFIA

Giacomo Devoto's etymological dictionary tells us that the word *mafia* is probably derived from the Arabic *mah_jas_*, meaning "boasting." It is presumed that the Saracens gave this name to the Sicilians who rebelled against their rule.

Whatever its origin, the fact is that the first signs of organized crime appeared in the early part of the 16th century at about the same time as Spain introduced the Inquisition into Sicily. These were small bands of Sicilians who had taken to banditry to protect the small people against the excesses of the Spanish government. Today many countries have their own homegrown form of this type of vicious organization, which extorts a cut from the sale of the product turned out by honest, self-respecting citizens. Sicily has been struggling for decades to rid itself of this parasite. Today with universal education and a rise in the standard of living, the mafia in Sicily is fast dropping to the role of petty crime.

WORLD WAR II TO THE PRESENT DAY

In just the past half century, Sicily has been successfully pulling itself up by the bootstraps. The economy, which had shown little improvement between 1860 and the end of Second World War, now shows a continuing annual growth rate. The European Common Market is offering the island new economic possibilities.

Sicily has been successful in attracting foreign capital by granting tax advantages. Within a short period, the number of corporations has risen from 218 to 1,576. Local laws favorable to prospectors have encouraged foreign companies to probe for oil. In

1953, Gulf struck oil near Ragusa linking it with pipelines to Augusta, the first refinery on the eastern coast.

The island's role increased to that of principal producer of oil in Italy with the discovery, by the Italian company, ENI, of another oil field in the sea off Gela. Sicily built four refineries to handle this new source of oil, as well as large quantities of crude oil imported from Russia, the Near East, and Libya. A pipeline built to connect an important discovery of methane gas in Gagliano would soon result in a new industry and jobs in Enna, one of the poorest Sicilian provinces. Other pipelines are being built throughout the island, according Sicily the cheap power it will need to make industrialization possible.

The discovery and refinement of oil has resulted in the building of a thermoelectric plant, a cement works, and factories for the production of fertilizers, plastics, and other petrochemical products. Gela, for the first time in a thousand years, has become an industrial center.

Sicily's transformation into a significant industrial part of Italy can be seen in every part of the island's economy. The number of tractors in use at the end of the Mussolini regime was under a thousand; by 1955 it had increased to five thousand. After the war, Augusta developed into the busiest Sicilian port. By 1964 it led Venice and Naples for tonnage handled, surpassing even Genoa as Italy's most important port. Agriculture, too, now has a new look. A greater variety of crops has been introduced, while modern techniques are now used in the cultivation of grapes and tomatoes. The age-old growth of lemons and oranges now exceeds that of any other Italian region. The island has doubled its production of potatoes and has multiplied by five times that of artichokes. Sicily produces one-eighth of the country's olive oil, while one-fourth of Italy's fishing boats sail from Sicilian ports. The island is fast becoming one of the country's most important producers of wine. It now has the most vineyards of any region and its production of wine is second only to that of Apulia, while many of its wines are being accepted among Italy's best.

Finally, the age-old separation of east and west, and of north and south has been brought to an end by the construction of ultra-modern superhighways that crisscross most of the island, giving access to its most remote corners. Radio, television, the telephone, the automobile, and, now the computer, have become part of every household and have succeeded in destroying one of Sicily's worst enemies—isolation.

Proud of their self-government, Sicilians have repudiated the mafia's association with drugs and prostitution. The classroom, for two millennia denied to ninety-seven percent of its people is now available to all of its citizens. No more than three percent of its population, mostly belonging to an earlier era, are illiterate. Now everyone can read, write, and speak Italian, which forms an important link to the peninsula and the country's past.

Sicilia—Quo vadis?

TOURISM

Sicily is seeking new industries suited to its people and its climate. It has found an excellent one in tourism. It was the northern Italians who first discovered Sicily as a gracious vacation land. In increasing numbers they found, at a reasonable cost, a mild climate; delicious food, so different from their own up north; comfortable accommodations; and hosts steeped in centuries of civility. Europeans and Americans are now making the same discovery. Tourism has become an important element of Sicily's growing economy.

FOLK POETRY

Alas, the Sicilian language is fast disappearing. Since 1875 not a single Sicilian grammar has been written in Sicily or anywhere in Italy. The first grammar to be produced in the 20th century was written in the United States by an American of Sicilian heritage. That grammar and a second one written by an American with no ethnic tie to Sicily are the island's only linguistic link to its past.

Although most Sicilians now speak Italian as their principal language, many of them are still bilingual. Contrary to the opinion expressed by those unfamiliar with Sicilian and by the many Sicilians themselves who, by weight of their demeaning past, have come to accept as inferior anything Sicilian, Sicily possesses a language which has a soft, feral beauty. Its hundreds and hundreds of poets have amply demonstrated this in poetry that remains at the folklore level and is still unpublished. But what has seen its way into print is sinuous, sonorous, and expressive of the Sicilian personality.

THE THEATER

In the early years of the 20th century, there surfaced a theatrical movement, a direct descendant of the *commedia dell'arte*, in which plays were written and performed, both comic and semi-comic, in the Sicilian language. It was a movement headed by a gifted poet, Nino Martoglio, whose tragic death in 1921 brought it to a sudden end. The great Sicilian dramatist Luigi Pirandello wrote some of his early masterpieces in Sicilian; these were later translated into Italian.

It was this same Luigi Pirandello (1867–1936) who dominated the world theater during the first half of the 20th century. Every play, written in Italian, was an immediate hit in Rome, Turin, Palermo, Buenos Aires, Rio de Janeiro, Berlin, Paris, and New York. Translated into all of the European languages, most of his prime dramas were made into movies. He wrote fifty-six plays, of which forty-four were in Italian and twelve in Sicilian. Pirandello was awarded the Nobel Prize in Literature in 1934.

SICILIAN POETS

Unknown to most literary critics and poetasters, Sicily has a large body of elegant poetry in Sicilian dating back to its emperor Frederick II. Because of its chaotic history, a large part of it was destroyed as the invading armies turned the cities to rubble. Much

Luigi Pirandello (1867–1936).

of it, however, found its way up into Tuscany in medieval and Renaissance archives. A good deal of it has been brought to light and published. There is much more to be uncovered.

It was Frederick II (*Stupor Mundi*, World Wonder), himself a poet, who brought together at his court in Palermo, in the 13th century, the first school of Italian poets, which came to be known as the Sicilian School. Modeled on the poetry of the southern French Troubadours, it invented the sonnet, so widely used by Dante, his contemporaries, and Petrarch. Dante tells us that his Florentine *dolce stil nuovo* poets used both the Troubadours and the Sicilian School as models.

In modern times, Salvatore Quasimodo (1901–1968), another Sicilian, was awarded the Nobel Prize in Literature in 1959. One of the outstanding Italian poets since Dante and Petrarch, had he not written poetry, he would be remembered as a gifted translator of Shakespeare, Molière, and Greek, Latin, and American classics.

Painting and Music

There were gifted painters and musicians, too. In the 15th century, Sicily's gifted artist, Antonello da Messina (*c.* 1430–1479), after having studied with the Dutch painters, is credited with having introduced new paint mediums to the Florentine painters. Alessandro Scarlatti (1659–1725), the founder of the Neapolitan School, developed some of the basic musical forms, including the overture. He composed 105 operas, 200 Masses, and over 700 cantatas and oratorios. Vincenzo Bellini during a short lifetime (1801–1835) wrote beautiful operas such as *Norma* and *La Sonnambula*, which are still a part of the repertory of every important opera house. His melodic style demands virtuosity of the singers.

Salvatore Quasimodo (1901–1968).

Vincenzo Bellini (1801–1835).

THE NOVEL

Some of Italy's outstanding novelists are Sicilian, many of whom have been translated into English. We'll mention one only, Giuseppe Tomasi, Duke of Palma and Prince of Lampedusa (1896–1957), whose *Il Gattopardo* (The Leopard) is ranked by most literary critics as the finest Italian novel ever written.

The Tomasis belonged to the last of a fading Sicilian aristocracy, which dates back to the Norman 11th century and which ended in 1860, when Garibaldi routed the Bourbons from Italy and lower Italy. Lampedusa depicts the period in Sicily when the fading old aristocracy was trying to find a place in the new bourgeois society.

Epilogue as Prologue

There you have it, the history of the first civilized people of the Western world, for two millennia enslaved by foreign masters. First settled by Ancient Greece around 700 B.C., it developed into the jewel of the Western world, with a highly productive agriculture, with poets, philosophers, mathematicians, scientists, and dramatists, whose plays were performed in coliseums more active than those in the mother country. At its apogee Greek Sicily could boast a civilization superior to that of Athens, which in envy tried and failed to bring it to heel. Many others, however, did succeed in invading it, in stealing its natural wealth and accumulated treasures, and in enslaving its people.

Why Sicily? Because of its location, in the middle of the Mediterranean, between Europe and Africa, it was within easy grasp of foreign invaders. From ancient times to modern, Sicilians have been a gentle people wanting only to cultivate their land and live in peace. With the exception of the Ancient Greeks, the Arabs, and the Normans, all invaders have stolen from Sicily and given nothing back. The worst was Spain, whose rule, the cruelest in Sicilian history, struck fear into the hearts of the helpless islanders.

When Spain seized control of Sicily, it found there a large number of Arabs and Jews, all productive members of society. The Arabs had developed and continued to maintain the most fruitful agriculture in the Mediterranean basin, while the Jews were the island's finest craftsmen and physicians. The Spanish Inquisition murdered them all in a planned genocide. By the 17th century there were no more Jews or Arabs left in Sicily. The few who survived had managed to escape to the Italian peninsula.

It was the same royal house of Spain, which through its viceroy, its army, and the Inquisition, decimated the population—excessive taxes, injustice, starvation, and burning at the stake. By the 17th century the only wealthy landowners in Sicily were the viceroy, the members of the Inquisition, who had kept for themselves the confiscated wealth of their victims, and a few favored, fawning native sycophants, brought into the royal club by Spanish royalty.

In a rage, the people fought starvation through banditry. History has lost count of the hundreds of Robin Hoods who stole from the rich to keep the people alive. Spain was mainly responsible for spawning a class of criminals that soon developed into the organized crime syndicate known today as the mafia. It is a cruel irony that the very people who have suffered for centuries from this outlaw class are now called *mafiosi*.

The Sicilian language does not possess a future tense; the future is indicated by the vivid present. "I do it tomorrow," Sicilians will say, not "I shall do it tomorrow," for they have known from the beginning of time that there would never be a tomorrow. Whenever calamity strikes, Sicilians will shrug their shoulders and say *È u destinu*, "it is destiny—God's will," for they have known, through the ages, that it was always foreigners, not they, who were masters of their destiny. Little wonder that it is only with fingers crossed that Sicilians will say, "Free, at last!"

View of Catania with Mount Etna hovering above.

Index

Page numbers in *italics* denote illustration.